UPCYCLING

Create Beautiful Things with the Stuff You Already Have

By Danny Seo

Photographs by Jennifer Levy

RUNNING PRESS
PHILADELPHIA · LONDON

Published by Running Press,
A Member of the Perseus Books Group

Printed in China

ISBN 978-0-7624-4179-2
Library of Congress Control Number: 2011923369

E-book ISBN 978-0-7624-4358-1

9 8 7 6 5 4 3 2 1
Digit on the right indicates the number of this printing

Photographs by Jennifer Levy
Cover and interior design by Jason Kayser
Edited by Jennifer Kasius
Typography: Eames Century Modern and Benton Sans

Photo on p. 28: ©iStockphoto.com/Jean Assell

Running Press Book Publishers
2300 Chestnut Street
Philadelphia, PA 19103-4371

Visit us on the web!
www.runningpress.com

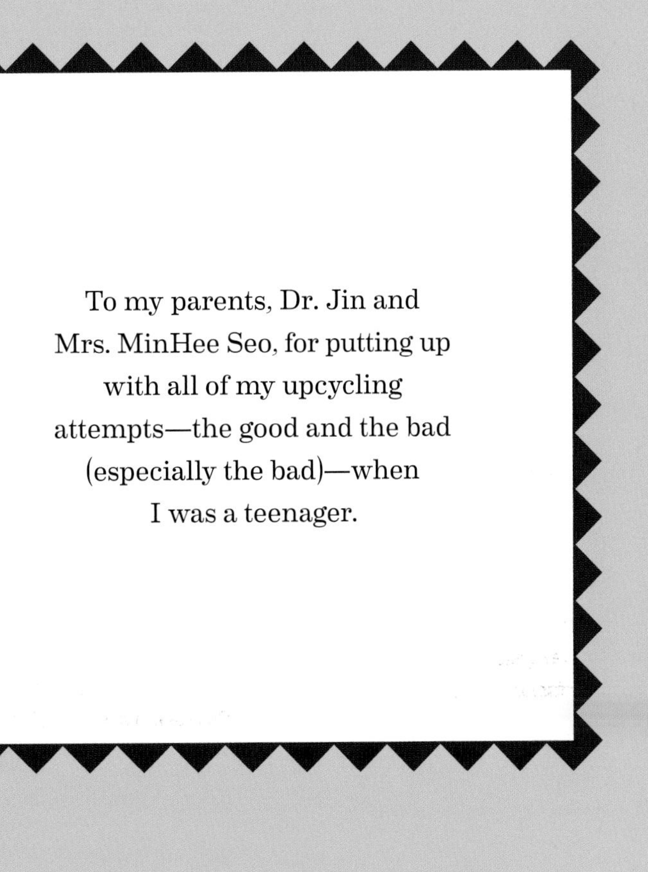

To my parents, Dr. Jin and Mrs. MinHee Seo, for putting up with all of my upcycling attempts—the good and the bad (especially the bad)—when I was a teenager.

Contents

10
Coca-Cola

Introduction

Imagine you're at your doctor's office with an ailment—a persistent cough, dizziness, a cramping in the hands—and you finally get a diagnosis that gives your condition a name. Even though you're still suffering, at least there's some comfort in knowing whatever it is you have, it has a name, and you're on the path to curing it. I kind of felt the same way with my years of recycling trash and everyday objects into better, brighter, and cooler things and finally learning what it was I was actually doing.

For years, I've worked as both an interior designer and magazine editor where I've done everything from transforming a celebrity's home from boring to sexy boudoir, to producing magazine stories on creating the perfect Thanksgiving table settings using stuff you might have around the house. My philosophy toward doing it yourself was never about buying lots of stuff or supplies, but about making do with what you have and using basic skills to create extraordinary results. It wasn't quite recycling, and it wasn't quite crafting; it was what I called a hybrid of MacGyver (the resourceful TV spy)-meets-HGTV. Anyway, my diagnosis for what I did for a living came in the form of an e-mail from a producer at NBC's *Today*: after seeing everything I've done over the years, she wanted to book me to do a segment about upcycling. So now it was official—I was an upcycler.

Think of upcycling as a higher form of recycling. When you upcycle, the end result is far better than the material's intended purpose, and you end up with something that's pretty darn cool and all your own creation. Beware of its close cousin but polar opposite: *downcycling*. For example, a Tide bottle recycled into a bird feeder is what I call downcycling: it's still ugly, probably reeks of detergent, and no bird really wants to stick their head inside to feed from sticky seed. However, a plastic water bottle that is cut, manipulated, and painted to look like the most magical flower that might live, say, in Wonderland (see page 188) is *upcycling*.

As an interior designer, I've worked with celebrities who have multimillion-dollar bank accounts and want me to create comfortable homes that reflect their unique style. Since I'm also an environmentalist, they know that everything will be as eco-friendly as possible. For many that may mean custom-upholstered hemp sofas, reclaimed-wood end tables, and crushed-recycled-concrete countertops for the kitchen. But to me that also means salvaging from thrift stores and flea markets. So the celebrity homes you may have seen me decorate in the pages of *InStyle* or *O: The Oprah Magazine* feature tons of upcycling ideas that cost next to nothing to make: glass bottles made into vases, or an old

IKEA light fixture found in the trash made into a charming birdcage chandelier (see page 24 to see what I mean!). Great style doesn't have to mean great big budgets; on the contrary, beautiful homes are created using ingenious decorating techniques, most of which cost very little to do.

As a magazine editor, my job has been to travel the country and find homes that are interesting and are decorated from a very specific point of view in the most beautiful way imaginable. The very best photos I've ever produced are the ones that feature nearly zero-cost ideas. One of my favorites involved a "collection" table filled with all sorts of found objects from nature: from oversized pinecones to dried mushrooms with tiny phrases carved into them. You just can't buy this from a store, and it makes a home, well, your home. These are the kinds of things I'm interested in creating.

Many people ask how I got started on this crafty path, and when I really think about it, it goes all the way back to when I was a child. In the seventh grade, I wanted to drive the message home to my peers that "throwing away" trash didn't mean it magically disappeared, but went to an overflowing landfill. So I got permission to fill all the display cases in our school with trash I collected from around the school in layers of paper, plastic, metal, and cardboard. Not only did it look like a modern work of art, it was also a cool way to get the message across. Unfortunately, it also became accidental gossip fodder for my classmates. One of the glass cases contained a breakup note from a girl who had intended to send it to her boyfriend and then had a change of heart and threw it away. The crinkled note was unfurled and pressed against the glass for all to read. Oops . . .

In my high school years, I ran a national environmental organization called Earth 2000 and campaigned all over the world on behalf of our planet's natural resources. But on weekends, the activist hat came off, and my inner crafter came out: I was probably the only teenage regular at our local flea markets, swap meets, and Goodwill store who wasn't dragged there by their mother. In my parents' basement, I reupholstered chairs I'd found on the streets with argyle sweaters, made colorful garlands out of beach sea glass, and recycled brown-paper grocery store bags into marbleized gift wrap.

Now in my thirties, I've made a career out of my passion for environmental concerns, combined with my love of crafting. And now I know it has a name: *upcycling*. With this book, I hope you'll be inspired to see that it doesn't take a lot of skill, money, or resources to make beautiful and decorative accessories, gifts, artwork, centerpieces. Instead, you'll be able to use things you already have. Not only can you achieve gorgeous-looking results that don't take a lot of time, but you can proudly say you did it yourself. Added bonus: you don't need to buy complicated crafting tools. In a way, I've given all of these upcycling projects a big ol' KISS: Keep It Simple, Sam.

In an increasingly disposable world, I think it's empowering to make something yourself and even reassuring that something you no longer use doesn't necessarily have to be shipped to a landfill. There's something calming and meditative about sitting down and tapping into your own imagination—and not Google—to come up with fantastic ideas on how to give something new life, new meaning, or a new use. Yes, we're crafting, and yes, we're being eco-friendly, but we're also taking control at the same time, too.

Creating *Upcycling* was an absolute joy that brought back so many childhood memories. It's a culmination of the best of the best, and I hope you'll try each and every project, and be inspired to invent your own.

Happy Upcycling!

—Danny Seo

Sharpie
WESTCOTT
CRAFTSMAN
USA
E6000
CAUTION
INDUSTRIAL STRENGTH
MADE IN CHINA

Materials for Upcycling

I'm often asked what are the essential tools any upcycler should have in their arsenal. In an ideal world, we'd all have a giant craft room that's completely outfitted with every imaginable tool neatly lined up, every shade of craft paint, and rows of unfinished wood blocks, frames, and trays ready to be embellished and upcycled. The reality is this: you *could* spend thousands of dollars by filling up your shopping cart at the craft store, but I guarantee you will still find yourself missing something. So instead of preparing for a craft-a-palooza, start with the basics and forget the rest. When you do decide to upcycle that cashmere sweater into a patchwork quilt, then go buy the specialty tools you need to make it happen.

Here are my essentials that I think every upcycler will need. The best part is that these are easy to find and inexpensive. Always go for quality, not quantity.

1. Sharp Scissors: It's very tempting to reach for the ten-pack of colorful scissors for $10 at the craft store, but bypass it. Sharp scissors are the key to getting professional results, so splurge and get the best you can afford. Fiskars brand is my choice because the blades are coated with titanium nitride for strength and durability. Not only have I been able to cut clean, sharp lines into paper, but I've been able to slice through rope, twine, leather, and other tough materials with ease.

2. Glue Gun: My favorite place to buy a professional glue gun isn't the craft shop, but the home improvement store. Don't go for the pocket-size, pink-colored "just-for-women" kind; go for the heavy-duty-contractor one instead. Get an industrial-strength gun that heats up quickly, delivers an even amount of hellishly hot glue, and can be propped to stand upright when not in use without leaking out any melted glue.

3. X-Acto Knife: Whenever your scissors are either too big to cut an intricate design or you need to puncture something like a plastic bottle, an X-Acto knife is the way to go. While you're at it, pick up a self-healing mat at the craft store to do all of your paper-cutting projects on. It'll protect your tabletop surfaces and make cutting smoother, cleaner, and easier.

4. E-6000 Glue: Obsessed is the understatement of the century for how I feel about this adhesive. It's pretty much evident throughout this entire book that I've found 1,001 uses for this glue. And to be clear: I don't own stock. Whenever I need to glue something together when I know hot glue won't do the trick, I reach for my tube of E-6000. This industrial-strength glue takes about twenty-four hours to fully dry, but it does one impressive job joining materials together. I could glue an itty-bitty teacup to a heavy ceramic plate with this stuff and hold the two together by the handle of the teacup.

5. White Craft Glue: I use this stuff all the time for projects when I don't have to worry about making a superstrong hold. Choose whatever brand you either like or is the cheapest; in my book, craft glues are all the same. Whether you're glittering or gluing cut-outs onto paper, a squeezable bottle of craft glue is a must-have material.

6. Foam Brushes: At Michaels craft stores, you'll often see foam craft brushes in all sorts of sizes on sale for next to nothing. I love to buy them in bulk and store in a large jar in my craft room. They are indispensable for painting unfinished wood surfaces, spreading a light adhesive for silver leafing, decoupaging paper, or anything that calls for a brush. I've even painted the edges of my wall with them.

7. Goof Off: Walk down the paint aisle at your home improvement store and pick up a bottle of Goof Off. This stuff is great for getting sticky labels off of bottles: if you're upcycling a wine or spirits bottle for a project, those labels can be a complete pain in the you-know-what to remove. Goof Off makes it a breeze. If you accidentally get paint on a tabletop, just squirt some Goof Off, let it saturate, and wipe it right off. I could go on about the thousands of uses for Goof Off, but this I know for sure: one little bottle will last you a very long time.

8. Cordless Drill with Bits: I have power and hand tools that I purchased that still have the security seal still intact on the box. My cordless drill, on the other hand, is used pretty much every single day. Invest in the best drill you can possibly buy, and make sure you have two rechargeable batteries for it; while one battery is being used, the other one can be charging as a backup. Nothing is worse than being halfway through a project and realizing the drill has lost all its juice. Buy all the necessary bits to go with your drill: flat head and Phillips head screw bits and a box of titanium drill bits in a variety of sizes to drill holes into all types of surfaces.

9. Staple Gun: If there's one thing that every prop stylist has in their tool box, it's the staple gun. Want to hang up Christmas lights in a café-light pattern outdoors? Staple gun. Need to reupholster a chair using an old sweater? Staple gun it into place. Want to make a mini-house using book jackets as roof shingles? Yep, staple gun. Fast, powerful, and easy.

10. Alphabet Stamp Kit and Permanent Ink Pad: Customization and personalization are two key ways to make any upcycling project uniquely yours or perfect for giving. Since my handwriting is just above the visual excellence of, say, a six-year-old's penmanship, I prefer to use alphabet stamps to spell out names or phrases. They come in a variety of different font styles at the craft store and in all sorts of sizes; choose the style and size that works best for you. I have just one ink pad: a black, permanent, indelible pad. Why on earth they make other pads with inks that smudge and easily wipe off is beyond me; make sure you get the pads that leave permanent impressions that are absolutely, positively smudge-free.

11. Needle Nose Pliers: Needle nose pliers are your crafting tweezers; you can use it to bend the finest wire into loops and closures. You can grab the thinnest needle and thread it through with ease. It will be that occasional tool you'll be glad you have when you realize you really need it.

12. Florist Wire and Tape: I'm the kind of person who buys a bouquet of flowers from the supermarket, unwraps it, and just tosses it into a glass vase with water and hopes for the best. But still, I find florist wire and tape indispensable for nonflower-arranging needs. The wire is great for twisting and bending when making paper or plastic flowers; the tape is fantastic for taking a crazy mess of stray wires from a project and wrapping them all together neatly and easily. Both materials are dirt cheap, so grab some and keep them handy.

13. Double-Stick Tape: When you want to attach two piece of paper together, thin strips of double-stick tape are a simple way to achieve the task. Glue isn't always the solution as an adhesive, and single-sided tape just can't get the job done. Keep your double-stick tape in its own Ziploc bag; leaving it out in the open is just asking dirt, dust, and pet hair to attach itself to your tape roll.

14. Sewing Kit: I don't sew, and I have, perhaps, an irrational fear of sewing machines. This fear is that I'll sew all of my fingers together when I manage to lose control between the speed of the needle and the pedal. Anyway, if you don't share a fear of the machine but are fearful of the hundreds of dollars it costs to buy one, a basic sewing kit can do in a pinch. Budget saver: save several hotel sewing kits in your arsenal. Splurge: invest in several spools of string, sewing needles, and a seam cutter.

15. Twine: A big spool of uncoated, all-natural twine can be used for an almost endless number of projects. Tie-dye some sheets? Make knots with twine. Need a make-do drying line outdoors to air-dry your just-dyed sheets? Run some twine between two trees. Want to hang up an upcycled pendant light? Use a few pieces of twine twisted together.

Performix

PAKSLEY
BASIL

CHAPTER ONE:

Upcycling Ideas for Decorating

When I was nineteen years old, I left my parents' home in Reading, Pennsylvania for Washington, DC where I worked as a part-time lobbyist for a non-profit environmental group while simultaneously writing my very first book about my teenage activism years. Living on my own, I was intent on having a studio apartment that was beautifully decorated and looked grown-up. But with modest means, that also meant I couldn't go to a fancy furniture store and buy all new pieces.

Instead, I slowly searched for bargains at local flea markets, thrift shops, and even Dumpster-dived when other tenants would move out of my apartment building. My first upcycling project as a first-time tenant involved an old church pulpit I found on the street: I took it home, painted it with three coats of gray paint, added wheels, and turned it into a TV stand. The shelves on the back that once held Bibles now held cassette tapes and DVDs, which could be easily accessed by simply wheeling the podium forward. I called it sacrilegious chic.

I still have that TV stand today, and it just goes to show that with a little elbow grease and ingenuity, timeless pieces can be created with very little money. Upcycled items for the home aren't just economical; they can also be one-of-a-kind pieces that add character to one's home. While it's tempting to order everything on the pages of a catalog when it comes to decorating your home, why would you? If your family and your home are unique to you, why decorate it in a generic, one-size-fits-all style? It doesn't take much to turn a ho-hum room into one that could easily be photographed for the pages of a magazine. Try an upcycled rug, a collection of upcycled decorative accessories, or make an upcycled pillow for the boring sofa you've been thinking about replacing. Think of these handmade items like sprinkles: sure a cupcake on its own tastes good, but that dash of sprinkles makes the experience even better.

Bear-"Skin" Oriental Rug

SUPPLIES: Used oriental rug (any size), sharp scissors (I like the Fiskars brand), hot glue gun with extra glue sticks, permanent marker, any kind of thin rope that coordinates with the color of rug you're upcycling.

You know that chain-store oriental-style rug that's been rolled up and stashed away in the basement for the past five years? Upcycle it into a whimsical bearskin rug with just a few simple tools. The more ornate and—I can't believe I'm writing this—tacky the rug is, the better the finished result will be. A good tip: if you pick up a used rug from a flea market or thrift store, be sure to have it professionally cleaned to remove any traces of possible bed bugs, dust mites, and other allergens. If it's winter, you can always leave the rug outdoors overnight in below freezing temperatures; it'll literally freeze whatever's lurking inside to death. Just give it a good vacuuming before bringing it inside.

HOW-TO: Flip the rug upside down on the floor so you're working on the back side. ➔ Using a permanent marker, trace the shape of a bearskin rug, using as much of the surface as possible to get the largest finished rug. If you mess up, no worries; just adjust your silhouette with the marker until you're happy; you'll never see the back side anyway, so keep tracing until it looks like a bearskin rug. ➔ Using sharp scissors, cut the shape of the rug and discard the scraps. ➔ To prevent fraying, use a hot glue gun to adhere rope around the perimeter of the rug.

Birdcage Chandelier

SUPPLIES: Paper covered pendant light (I used an IKEA "Rutbo" fixture), chicken wire (available in the gardening section at any Lowe's store), silver florist wire, scissors, wooden branches from the yard, artificial birds (from any Michaels craft store).

I get inspiration from all sorts of places, and one of my favorites is high-end furnishing stores. On one visit, I spied a copper-gilded chandelier with charming silk artificial birds resting on branches inside. What's the price tag for this French-made illumination? $1,000. Even though I was decorating a celebrity client's home and using her box office mucho money to buy things, my inner gut just couldn't waste a cool thousand on something I could make myself. Here's my version that comes at a 95 percent reduction in cost, is a total cinch to make, and still conjures up ooh-la-la.

HOW-TO: Any hardwired pendant light fixture with a paper shade cover will do, so try to use one you already have or source one from a flea market or online before buying a new one to upcycle. ➔ Rip the paper off completely, leaving the metal-wire ribs intact on the fixture. ➔ Carefully wrap chicken wire around the light fixture to create the "cage," bending the edges of the chicken wire onto the ribs and reinforcing it with bits of twisted florist wire. ➔ Trim the excess with scissors. ➔ Insert branches so they securely rest inside the light fixture and attach birds using the existing wire or clips on their feet. You can also use a hot glue gun to secure them in place. ➔ Be sure to use the recommended wattage lightbulb or—better yet—invest in energy-efficient LED bulbs that do not get hot and are not a fire hazard.

Ceramic-Dipped Silk Flowers and Plastic Fruit

SUPPLIES: Silk flowers and plastic fruit (flea markets, eBay, and your grandmother's basement are good place to find them), Faster Plaster powdered plaster, Styrofoam block (save old packaging when you buy something like a new TV).

When I first started developing projects for *Upcycling*, this was the very first successful project that I felt met the mission of the overall book. The end result is unexpected, and the process is ludicrously easy and fun to do. Even though it's a project I came up with early on, it still remains one of my favorites because it transforms something most people find universally unappealing—fake flowers and plastic fruit—and upcycles them into something spectacular: ceramic-looking sculptures.

HOW-TO: Pull the leaves off of the silk flowers leaving you with just the flower heads on their original stems; discard the leaves. ➔ Mix the Faster Plaster in a bowl according to package instructions, making sure the wet plaster is lump-free and slightly runny. ➔ Dip the flowers one by one, swirling each flower in the plaster mixture, making sure to cover the petals completely; shake the flower over the bowl to remove the excess plaster mixture. ➔ Insert the stem of the flower into the Styrofoam block and allow it to dry. Depending on the color of the flower, you may need to re-dip it; the darker the color, the more dips will be required to completely cover it. For plastic fruit, spoon the mixture over each entire piece until covered. ➔ Stand it upright on a Styrofoam block for drying. ➔ Use excess plaster mixture to cover a thrift store wicker basket by pouring it all over the basket. ➔ Allow everything to dry (about 2 hours) before arranging.

String Outdoor Seating

SUPPLIES: Old aluminum chaise lounge or chair, Valspar Signature Colors Brilliant Metals spray paint (available at Lowe's; I used silver), one 50-inch strand of 100-percent-cotton outdoor rope (the same kind to make an outdoor clothes drying line), scissors.

Before

There's a vicious cycle that needs to end when it comes to spring cleaning time. Piles of aluminum outdoor furniture with PVC plastic strips appear at the end of driveways, covered in dirt, mildew, and remnants of the harsh winter. Out the dirty pieces go and in come replacement furniture from the home improvement store. We buy them because they are cheap, lightweight, and disposable. The insanity, my friends, needs to end. With some simple rope, scissors, and a can of spray paint, you can rehabilitate your own furniture (or rescue one from your neighbor's trash heap) to make this ultracool, ultracomfy outdoor seating chaise.

HOW-TO: Use sharp scissors to cut off the PVC straps from the outdoor chair. ➜ Wipe the aluminum frame with a damp towel to remove any residual dirt or debris. ➜ Once it's dry, spray a light coat (outdoors or in a well-ventilated area) of the Valspar spray paint all over the frame. Keep spraying additional light coats until the chair is completely and evenly painted. ➜ Once it's completely dry, knot the rope into place at the top of the chair and begin tightly wrapping the rope over and under the entire frame of the chair. Once you reach the base of the chair, tie another knot to secure it into place. ➜ Trim both knots with scissors, and use a match to burn the ends so it doesn't fray.

Chinatown-Tote-Bag Shower Curtain

SUPPLIES: Three 22 × 26-inch tote bags (available at pearlriver.com), small scissors or a seam ripper, a hot glue gun, a grommet kit.

In my early twenties, I was a magazine editor in New York City working on a new publication called *Organic Style* that celebrated stylish, eco-friendly living. Part of my job was to seek out new trends, styles, and products that were cutting-edge and interesting to our readers, including cool, new reusable bags that replaced throwaway plastic ones. I remember seeing these colorful, plaid tote bags carried by all sorts of people during my walks through Chinatown. These inexpensive bags were used by people to carry everything from groceries to laundry to and from stores and their apartments. Over the years, these oversized, cheap tote bags have become an essential tool for stylists, since they can hold a lot of supplies and props without the risk of tearing. Even influential fashion designers have noticed their iconic, simple design: Marc Jacobs monogrammed some of the totes and used them as accessories in his collection for Louis Vuitton. Yes, the makers of the bags that are popular in Chinatown, where fake Louis Vuitton bags are often produced, have had their everyday bag copied by the man behind Louis Vuitton. What comes around, goes around, folks! Here's my take on the Chinatown tote bag: a classic-country shower curtain.

HOW-TO: A typical shower curtain is 72 × 72 inches, so use that as a measurement guide when making this project. Since math isn't my forte, I simply used an old shower curtain as a template and laid the ripped open bags on top to make the right size. ➔ Use a seam ripper to remove all the seams and handles off the tote bags, making sure to not rip any holes or tears into the bag. ➔ Lay out all three flat pieces of fabric on the ground and measure 75 inches across and 72 inches down; the extra 3 inches across is to allow for overlapping the three panels on top of each other. ➔ Using a hot glue gun, adhere the panels together, making sure to be generous with the glue for a very secure finish. ➔ Add twelve ½-inch brass grommets on the top, evenly spaced, according to the kit's instructions.

Heaven-on-Earth Bedroom Clouds

SUPPLIES: Old bed pillow, twine, thumbtack.

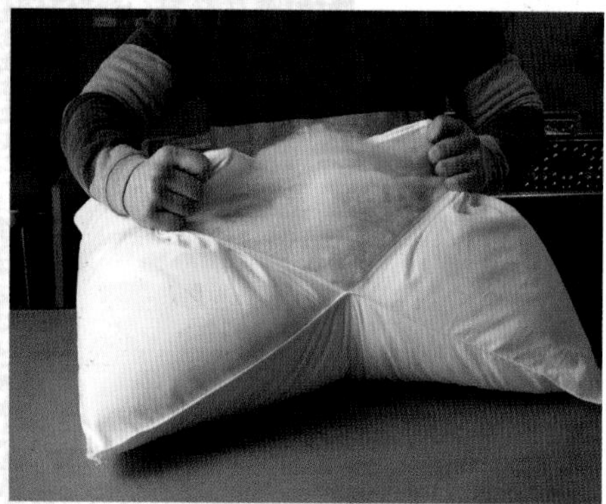

When I purchased a mid-century, modern home a few years ago and began the exhaustive renovations, I thought instead of ripping everything out and putting everything new inside, I would keep some of the character embellishments I found untouched. In the living room, giant waxed balls were stuck to the high ceilings; according to my neighbors, when the original homeowners had wine and cheese parties, they'd ball up the wax the cheese came encased in and—BAM!—up they went onto the ceiling. Thirty years later, the waxed balls remain, and their story is retold.

In the bedrooms, I found vintage glow-in-the-dark stars stuck to the ceiling that I could've easily peeled off, but decided to keep. To keep the whimsy alive, I thought these fluffy clouds would make it extra special when my niece and nephew visit.

HOW-TO: Simply rip open an old bed pillow filled with synthetic polyester stuffing, rip out large clumps, and tie a piece of twine around it. ➔ Then hang it from the ceiling with a thumbtack—so simple and so heavenly.

Fine-Tooth-Comb Bookshelf

SUPPLIES: Two 48-inch aluminum carpet Z-Bars (in the carpet supply section at the home improvement store), six small pocket combs, three ¾-inch U-bolt zinc pipes (at the home improvement store), six 1-inch plastic screw anchors with matching metal screws, twelve ¾-inch small binder clips in stainless (from any office supply store), cordless drill.

I was buying TSA-friendly toiletries to replenish my travel kit at my local Target store when I realized I didn't have a pocket comb. Looking at the selection of combs, I started playing with the bristles and wondered if they'd be strong enough to hold a paperback book. Yes, folks, this is how my mind works, even when I'm shopping at Target. So off I went to the book section and started gripping trashy romance paperbacks with the combs; they gripped so securely and beautifully. I figured a whole row of these on a wall could store, stack, and display paperback books in a beautiful and sculptural way.

HOW-TO: Choose a wall that can accommodate a 48-inch-long comb bookshelf. ➔ Mount two 1-inch plastic screw anchors in the wall at the beginning of the bookshelf; place the U-bolts on top of the mount and secure them into place by screwing the metal screws through the U-bolt openings. ➔ Repeat in the middle and end of the shelf area. ➔ Run both Z-Bars through all three U-bolts, making sure the Z-Bars are laying flat on top of each other. ➔ Insert the combs in between both Z-Bars, clipping them securely by using the stainless binder clips. ➔ Once done, remove the metal hooks on the binder clips by squeezing them out of the clips. ➔ To attach your books, gently wiggle them into the comb and let go.

A Quick, No-Nonsense Approach to
Learning the Basics of DOS
FRIENDLY DOS
OPERATING SYSTEMS

Wine-Cork Bath Mat

SUPPLIES: About 500 wine corks, a large shadow box (I used one designed to hold a flag), cork shelf liner.

If several years ago you took your doctor's advice that a glass of wine a day may be good for your health, hopefully you've saved enough wine corks to upcycle them into this totally adorable bath mat. Cork makes a wonderful surface to rest your freshly washed feet on because it's soft and porous and absorbs water without developing smelly mold or mildew. If you don't have hundreds of wine corks, that's no reason to start boozing it up: become friendly with your local wine bar, restaurant, or vineyard and ask them to collect used corks for you. You'd be surprised how easy it is to amass a collection.

HOW-TO: Pop out the glass front of the shadow box, and save it for a different upcycling project. ➔ Line the inside of the shadow box with layers of cork shelf liner until it's thick enough for a wine cork to reach the top of the shadow box when standing upright. ➔ Fill the shadow box with wine corks making sure to maximize the number of corks possible inside the box so they're snug, but not crammed into the box.

Gemstone Cabinet Knobs

SUPPLIES: Old knob, mineral or rock, E-6000 glue, low-adhesive painter's tape.

Two decorating secrets in updating a kitchen on a dime are to change the color of the walls with a fresh coat of paint and swap out dated cabinet knobs with new ones. In my kitchen, you don't have to do the tedious task of unscrewing each knob to give them a fresh look. Upcycle your old knobs with a colorful collection of geodes, sea glass, or minerals and ultrapowerful glue.

HOW-TO: Using E-6000 glue (available at Michaels craft stores), squeeze a generous amount onto the front of the knob and attach a mineral or rock onto its front. Don't try to use a different brand of glue for this project, no matter how powerfully strong it may promise on the package. I've used them all, and E-6000 is the best of the best for this. ➔ Using low-adhesive painter's tape, secure the rock onto the knob so it doesn't slide off as it dries. ➔ Allow it to dry for a full twenty-four hours and remove the tape.

Painter's-Tape Privacy Screen

SUPPLIES: Window or door and a few rolls of painter's tape.

Good fences may make good neighbors, but a restricted budget can prevent most of us from acting on this famous proverb. One simple way to add privacy to a window without resorting to heavy drapes and blinds that block the light is to use a few rolls of inexpensive painter's tape.

HOW-TO: Start by running tape evenly, both vertically and horizontally, on the window or door that you want to cover. ➔ Then run the tape diagonally so it crosses the intersections where the tape meets; the more that you add, the more interesting the design becomes, creating a kaleidoscope design that's both intricate and monotone. I like using the simple khaki-colored tape because it's light enough to allow more light in and simple enough in color to not look jarring, but feel free to experiment with other colors of tape if you want something more daring in your room.

Glittering Bad Artwork

SUPPLIES: Painting, white craft or glittering glue, small brush, small containers (I upcycled a cardboard egg carton), glitter.

Artwork doesn't have to be serious, and it doesn't have to be expensive either. Yard sales, flea markets, and your attic are great places to find inexpensive oil paintings that are perfect for this project. Don't use an expensive painting for this project. No matter how beautiful the end result may be, a glittered *Mona Lisa* is a gutted one.

With just a little bit of glue and glitter, you can add some unexpected sparkle, fun, and dimension to the simplest of paintings.

HOW-TO: Brush the glue on sections of the portrait you want glittered, and pour the glitter on top until these areas are completely covered. ➔ Tap off the excess glitter, and wait a few minutes for it to dry. ➔ Repeat these steps if you want to add additional colors or layers of glitter onto the portrait. ➔ Try mixing darker glitter with lighter hues in small batches to add dimension to the portrait, like I did here on the portrait of the older gentleman. Try this technique on landscapes and other paintings, too.

Gold-"Dipped" Plates

SUPPLIES: Ceramic plates, painter's tape, and one can of Krylon Brilliant Metals spray paint in Gold.

When doing research for *Upcycling,* I spent a lot of time looking for inspiration in both museums and retail stores. It wasn't until I stumbled into the store Moss in New York City's SoHo district that I realized I walked into a combination of both. Owner Murray Moss opened the gallery space to celebrate industrial product design with an eclectic mix of home furnishings and vintage pieces all uniquely displayed in museum-like cases with the twist you could actually purchase the items. Think being at the Metropolitan Museum of Art and Macy's at the same time.

In one case were blue and white ornate ceramic plates, dipped in real gold. The mix of the organic, dipped gold with the traditional plate created an interesting juxtaposition that I just loved. What I didn't love was the sky-high price tag per plate. Inspired, I found an inexpensive way to upcycle chipped plates in just two simple steps.

HOW-TO: Tape off sections of the plate you *don't* want covered in gold paint; try stripes, zigzags, or different shapes. ➜ In a well-ventilated area, spray light coats of the metal spray paint all over the plate until the plate is covered in paint. ➜ Allow it to dry completely before peeling off the tape.

Another idea: Upcycle coffee mugs by taping off the top half of the mug and spray-painting the bottom half gold.

Necktie Wreath

SUPPLIES: Metal wreath frame, lots of tacky neckties, and straight pins.

When I was working with a group of stylists on creating the projects for this book, I'd often hold up an item I was having trouble upcycling and would ask, "What do you guys think we could do with this?" I swear, nine out of ten times, the answer would be "you could make a wreath." So I made it my mission to make sure there weren't any wreath projects in this book and broke my own rule when I saw this beauty come to life. Finding vintage neckties is a cinch: ask your father, rummage a thrift store, or put a notice on Freecycle.org that you're in need of lots and lots of tacky ties. To me, the more tacky and crazy the ties are, the better your wreath's overall look will be.

HOW-TO: To make it, it couldn't be easier: use a metal wreath frame (at Michaels craft stores) and wrap the necktie around it completely and pin it into place. ➜ Repeat these steps until the whole frame is covered.

Plastic-Bottle Hourglasses

SUPPLIES: Two identical plastic bottles (I used Method handwash and Scope mouthwash bottles), wine and champagne corks, a cordless drill with a 3⁄16-inch bit, small funnel, and colorful, craft-store fine sand.

One of the rules of *Upcycling* (sounds like the opening to *Fight Club*, doesn't it?) is that the end product needs to have a functional purpose to it. And I'll follow that with this one: rules are meant to be broken. If you make one of these plastic-bottle hourglasses, don't expect the trickling sand to last for an entire hour. Instead, be happy that plastic bottles that once held soap and mouthwash have been spared from the recycling bin and are now gorgeous do-it-yourself creations on your home office desk.

HOW-TO: Be absolutely sure the plastic bottles are thoroughly clean and bone-dry inside. ➔ Drill a 3⁄16-inch hole through the wine cork, and insert half of it into the bottle. ➔ For plastic bottles with larger openings, use a larger champagne cork. ➔ Insert a funnel into the other bottle, and pour sand into it. ➔ Remove the funnel, and insert the corked bottle on top to create an hourglass. ➔ Make sure it's snug; if it's a bit loose, add a little glue around the edges of the two bottles.

CD-Jewel-Case Frames

SUPPLIES: Large piece of artwork, CD jewel cases, scissors, double-stick Velcro.

It's interesting how fast-evolving technology has made many things that were once considered high-tech, now obsolete. Compact discs seem to be on this path, and many of us have amassed a collection of CDs in their plastic jewel cases that we have absolutely no idea what to do with. In *Upcycling*, I've found a solution for both the CD and plastic case, and this project deals strictly with the case.

HOW-TO: Start by finding an interesting, large piece of artwork: an oversized photograph, a vintage map, a movie poster you've never gotten around to framing. ➜ Pull out the printed jacket art inside one of the jewel cases and use it as a template; cut out squares from your artwork, and insert each square into each jewel case. ➜ Attach them one by one to the wall using double-stick Velcro. ➜ Create abstract pieces by taking out jewel cases here and there like I did with this map, or display the entire piece of artwork in its whole.

AAA
NOR TH & SOUTH
C AROLINA

Cassette-Tape Tissue Box

SUPPLIES: Twelve clear cassette tape covers and hot glue gun.

Leaving a box of tissues on the bathroom counter can be unsightly, but a box of Kleenex is a toiletry essential. Instead of buying a store-bought tissue box container, raid your stash of cassette tapes instead. The end result of this upcycling project is one that's both functional and unique and is an absolute cinch to make.

HOW-TO: Glue eight of the cassette tape covers together to create an open box on the top and bottom. ➔ Glue two cassette tape covers together to create the bottom, but do not glue them to the box; you'll need to keep this open so you can easily refill the tissue box. ➔ For the top, remove half of each cassette tape cover off, and glue them on top so you have a 1-inch opening on top. ➔ Remove the cardboard covering off the box of tissues, and carefully place the stacked tissues inside the cassette tape box; pull the top sheet through the top, and you're good to sneeze.

Stenciled Cabinet

SUPPLIES: Lace fabric or doilies, spray adhesive, contrasting latex spray paint, fabric glue (for lace pillows).

Lace fabric and handmade doilies can easily be best described as granny style, but these flea market staples are the perfect stencil to update an old dresser, cabinet, or table in minutes with a modern flair. With just a little bit of colorful spray paint and spray adhesive, you can embellish a boring piece of furniture with the intricate design of the fabric that looks more gorgeously grand than granny.

HOW-TO: Spray a light coat of spray adhesive on the furniture's surface you want to stencil. ➔ Lay the piece of lace fabric or doily on top, and use your fingers to press it down firmly. ➔ Spray a light coat of spray paint over the fabric, using a contrasting color to the existing color on the piece of furniture. Spray several coats of paint until you achieve the desired effect; remember that a little paint does go a long way. ➔ Peel off the fabric and allow it to dry.

To make the lace pillows, use a fabric glue to attach the doilies wherever you want on the pillow. ➔ Use small dots of glue all over the back of the doily, and press it into place; it's easier to work with a flat surface, so remove the pillow's insert if possible. ➔ Allow it to dry.

Cast-Iron Pipe Hooks and Towel Rack

SUPPLIES: For the bathroom hooks: ½-inch cast-iron 90 elbow piece, ½-inch opening cast-iron flange, ½-inch cast-iron nipple, drywall screw. For the towel rack: ½ × 30-inch cast-iron pipe; two ½-inch 90 elbow pieces, two ½-inch cast-iron connectors, two ½-inch opening flanges, drywall screws. Spray paint in color of your choice (I used Valspar Brilliant Metal in Silver).

On Sunday mornings, one of my favorite things to do is to visit open houses and see how my neighbors live. Sure, it's a bit nosy, but that's why they call it an open house: anyone can come and snoop around. I can always tell when a home is a "flip" house, basically a property that an investor purchased, did high-impact, low-cost renovations, and re-listed at a higher price in hopes of making a profit. How can I tell? Cheap bathroom fixtures. Chrome-"looking" hooks and towel racks that look like pricey metal ones but are really faux-metal plastic fixtures.

This isn't my case for breaking the bank on buying five-star quality bathroom fixtures—because you can get the durability of solid cast metal hooks and towel racks at a fraction of the cost by making it yourself. While many upcycling projects involve taking everyday trash and transforming it into something new, it can also mean taking inexpensive raw materials—especially from the hardware store—and giving them a lift into something unexpected, elegant, and new.

Down the plumbing aisle, I was drawn to the simplicity of these cast-iron plumbing pieces and loved how they can be simply twisted together to create all new pieces like these bathroom hooks and a towel rack.

HOW-TO: For the bathroom hooks, twist the 90 elbow piece into the flange, and twist the nipple into the exposed opening on the elbow piece. ➔ Spray with light coats of paint, and use a drywall screw to mount it into the wall. ➔ For the towel rack, twist the connect piece into a flange, followed by the 90 elbow piece and then the 30-inch cast-iron piece; repeat these steps. ➔ Paint with several coats of light paint and allow it to dry. Mount to the wall with drywall screws.

Leather-Belt Doormat

SUPPLIES: Approximately 10 to 12 vintage/thrift-store leather belts, leather hole puncher (from the craft store), hemp string, scissors, a large threading needle.

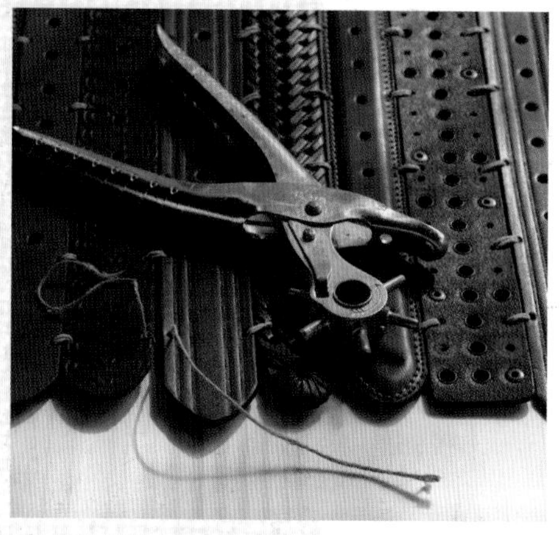

Several years ago, I had this crazy idea to upcycle vintage leather belts I found at a thrift store in Los Angeles into a briefcase. I used a leather hole puncher to cut small holes along the edges of the belt and connected them with hemp string. The project that I thought would only take a few hours ended up taking two weeks. I beat up my hands and got carpal tunnel syndrome because each pull of the hole puncher against the tough leather took a certain amount of strength to make a clean cut. But years later, the bag has been all over the world with me and back and still looks as good as the first day I used it. Nothing can take a beating like good, worn leather.

This project also involves leather belts, a hole puncher, and hemp string, but it's not as time-consuming (or painful) to create. Keep it by the front door or in front of the kitchen sink to stand on.

HOW-TO: Punch holes approximately every inch along the edge of two belts. ➔ Stitch them together using hemp string, knotting them at the beginning and end for extra reinforcement. ➔ If the belts are uneven in size, trim them along one edge with sharp scissors for a clean edge.

Starry-Sky Artwork

SUPPLIES: Landscape paintings (I found these two at a local flea market for $10 a piece), a small string of LED white lights (I used battery operated ones), a cordless drill with drill bits.

This might be one of the simplest projects in the entire book and perhaps the most magical. I was inspired by the world of Harry Potter. Remember the wall of paintings that come to life inside the school at Hogwarts? While I may not be able to have a portrait speak back to me, I can give life to a generic, flea-market painting by giving it a sparkling, starry sky in mere minutes.

HOW-TO: Start by drilling holes into the painting from the front of the painting; if there's any fraying, it'll show on the back and not the front. Be sure to use a cordless drill bit that will allow for the string light to poke through snugly, but not too large that it doesn't stay in place. You may need to start with smaller bit pieces and work your way up until you find the right size; I used a 7/32-inch drill bit for these paintings. ➔ Poke the lights through, turn on, and display.

Cork-Covered Lampshades

SUPPLIES: Lampshade, cork shelf-liner paper (found at Lowe's), X-Acto knife.

Shelf-liner paper can be found in any home improvement or kitchen supply store. It's a great material to use for a whole variety of projects because the adhesive is already on the paper, so you basically just peel and paste. I've used wood-grain, shiny, silver-colored, and all sorts of patterned paper for a wide variety of projects and, strangely enough, never once to line a single shelf.

Anyway, I also love shelf-liner paper because there's also a grid pattern on the back. That makes measuring easy because you can eyeball the size of paper you need and just cut along the premeasured lines to absolute perfection. No straight edge, X-Acto knife, or self-healing mat needed—just scissors and a steady hand.

HOW-TO: For this project, I upcycled an ugly lampshade into an illuminated one using genuine cork shelf-liner paper. Drum shell shades work easiest since you can cut out a rectangular piece of cork and just roll it along the shade. ➜ To make cut-outs in the cork, use an X-Acto knife to cut out whatever silhouette shapes you want first and then adhere it to the shade.

Holiday-String-Light Neon Artwork

SUPPLIES: 25-inch roll of plastic-coated electrical wire, florist wire, string of lights.

I've always been fascinated by neon artwork and have been drawn to modern art collections that feature artists who dabble in the medium. There's something unexpected about a large piece of neon hung on the wall in a gallery setting: it's bright, shiny, and colorful. While I'm not suggesting you smuggle a Budweiser light out of your favorite watering hole, I think it's safe to pull some inspiration from illuminated words for a fun upcycling project.

Here, I've taken unused string lights—these happen to be red from a Valentine's Day project—but any color will do. Spell out the word—perhaps "BOO!" for Halloween or "Noel" for Christmas.

HOW-TO: Use a 25-inch roll of plastic-coated electrical wire from the hardware store to twist into the word of choice. ➜ Use a little bit of florist wire to secure the string lights onto the finished electrical wire and then twist them around and around until the entire piece is covered.

Carpet-Sample Patchwork Rug

SUPPLIES: Approximately 100 carpet-sample squares, a roll of Rhino Grip double-sided carpet tape (in the carpet section of the home improvement store), scissors, a piece of heavy-duty canvas fabric the size of the finished rug.

I think I need to preface this project with a stern warning: do not go into your local hardware or flooring store and steal all of their free samples. Yes, the little squares of carpet are free for the taking, but they are intended for customers who are serious about making a wall-to-wall covering purchase. Instead, the next time you are making a flooring purchase or know someone who is making one, pick up your free samples then. The store gets the business they need, and you'll get the little squares of carpet to upcycle into this really fun rug.

HOW-TO: Lay the carpet samples on top of the canvas fabric, and design a pattern of your choice. ➔ Remove the samples and run rows of the carpet tape on the canvas. ➔ Add the carpet squares one sample at a time on top of the canvas, making sure to press firmly on the carpet so it adheres securely to the tape. ➔ Continue until the entire surface is covered. Use scissors to trim any excess fabric.

SUSAN WITTIG ALBERT
RUEFUL DEATH
K. L. GOING
SAINT IGGY

Plastic-Banana Fruit Bowl

SUPPLIES: Several plastic bananas, hot glue gun, spray paint.

There are certain things I see in people's homes or at flea markets that make me scratch my head and wonder why on earth they were ever created. One of them is plastic fruit. It's not like there was a sudden fruit crime spree where green grocers and chefs needed to trick thieves with faux fruit to prevent the real deal from getting stolen. Maybe people were tired of replacing rotten fruit from their kitchen countertops and thought faux fruit could free them up from visiting their supermarket. Who knows? All I know is that these things exist, so I made some into this ultracool fruit bowl.

HOW-TO: It couldn't be easier: just hot-glue several plastic bananas together. ➔ Use whatever spray paint color you want—I chose a metallic silver, but a creamy white would also look good—and coat the bananas with several layers of paint. ➔ Display real fruit in your fake fruit banana bowl.

Cozy Scarf-Blanket

SUPPLIES: Scarves of about the same length, iron-on Stitch Witchery tape, iron and ironing board, large needle and yarn (for heavier weight scarf-blanket).

It makes sense that something that makes you take the chill out of the air on the coldest of winter days would make you feel even warmer when multiplied. This upcycling project takes simple scarves and transforms them into a cozy throw that you can sleep with at night, cuddle under when watching a movie, or even travel with when inflight temperatures make you wonder if you're flying to the Arctic.

HOW-TO: If you want to make a no-sew blanket, lightweight scarves work best. These silk scarves are more decorative than warm and cozy, but they do a beautiful job at dressing up the drabbest of bedrooms. ➔ Use a medium-hot iron with no steam and strips of Stitch Witchery no-sew tape to attach the scarves together. ➔ Run a strip of tape along the edge of one scarf, lay another on top, and run the iron on top. It'll melt the tape and secure the scarves together. ➔ Repeat these steps until the entire blanket is made.

For a heavier weight scarf-blanket, you'll need a large needle and yarn; just hand-stitch two scarves together at a time until you've created a blanket in your desired size.

Reupholstered Pet Stairs

SUPPLIES: Throws or rugs, scissors, staple gun.

I have a reoccurring nightmare that I'm in some faraway place doing some fabulous photo shoot, and suddenly, I realize I haven't fed my dogs, and they've all died. I wake up (usually in a hotel room) and realize I don't have any dogs. And as much as I would love to adopt a few canine companions, I know my crazy schedule (and nightmares apparently) make it impossible. So I've become an uncle of sorts to my clients who are dogs owners. One thing I've noticed when I'm working on their homes is that many of them have pet stairs designed to help their furry friends climb in bed with their owners with ease. What's usually the problem with these stairways? They are—how do I put this delicately—ugly.

HOW-TO: To transform ho-hum stairs into chic ones like these only involves a flea-market score and a staple gun. ➔ Look for durable, colorful, intricately designed throws or rugs at flea markets, and staple gun them securely to the stairs. ➔ I used a vintage Peruvian blanket for these, but any colorful, boho-chic throw, rug, or blanket will do. ➔ Start with the actual stairs and trim the excess; use the scraps to cover the sides.

Safety-Pin Sequined Pillow

SUPPLIES: Pillow and safety pins (various shapes and colors).

This is an upcycling project that I designed to be featured in the pages of *O: The Oprah Magazine*, but it never made the final cut. I theorize it had something to do with the fact that the end result seemed a bit not-so-favorite-thing because of the sharp pins, even though the word "safety" preceded it. Nevertheless, I love it because it adds a starburst effect to any generic-looking pillow in just a matter of minutes and costs less than a dollar to make.

HOW-TO: To "sequin" a pillow, just use a variety of safety pins in different shapes and colors and secure them to the pillow. Make whatever pattern your heart desires.

Sharpie-Tie-Dyed Bedding and Napkins

SUPPLIES: Pillowcase, flat sheet, duvet cover, or napkin; Sharpie permanent marker; clothesline; rubbing alcohol (minimum 70 percent alcohol formula).

This upcycling project is appealing on so many levels because it's incredibly easy to do, it uses supplies most of us have on hand, and you end up with something really beautiful. I recommend practicing on an old pillow case or T-shirt before you break out the designer high-thread-count sheets because this project does involve a modicum of skill to pull off.

HOW-TO: Start by rubbing a Sharpie permanent marker along the edges of a pillowcase, flat sheet, duvet cover, or on a napkin; working with white fabric will achieve the best results. It should be a solid, thick, pen line, so rub carefully, slowly, and purposefully. ➔ Then on a clothesline outdoors, spray rubbing alcohol (minimum 70 percent alcohol formula) along the Sharpie line and watch it begin to bleed. The more alcohol you spray, the longer the streaks. ➔ Try mixing colors for a tie-dyed effect or keep it simple for a batik-inspired sheet set like I made here.

Fallen-Branch Shelves

SUPPLIES: Large branch, handsaw, cordless drill with bits, drywall screws and anchors, unfinished wood shelves.

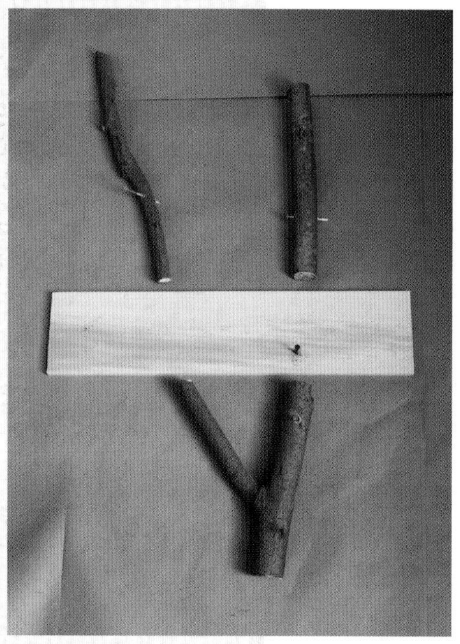

If a tree falls in the forest and no one is there to hear it, does it make a sound? My answer to this old philosophical question is quite simple: who cares? I'll upcycle the tree into a woodland-branch shelf.

HOW-TO: This upcycling project is part optical illusion; you'll need to cut the branch into four separate pieces and then reassemble them on the wall to look like one, consistent piece. ➜ Use a handsaw to cut the branches into pieces; one for the bottom, one for the middle, and two for the top. ➜ Attach the bottom piece to the wall by mounting drywall anchors into the wall, placing the branch on top of the anchors and screwing extra long screws through the branch and into the wall anchors for a firm, secure mount. ➜ Add a wood shelf on top and screw the shelf into place directly into the top of the branch. ➜ Repeat both steps until the branch shelf is complete.

Button-Silhouette Artwork

SUPPLIES: Prestretched artist canvas, black paint, paint-brush, white chalk, buttons, white craft glue.

The simple act of repairing a loose button on a piece of clothing seems to be an easy task lost on an entire younger generation. Whenever a button popped off a shirt or pants when I was a child, my mother would grab her jar of buttons and begin her mad task of finding a matching companion to fix it. Nowadays, instead of simply sewing a button on, we just toss it into the donation bag or, worse, throw it away. Jars of buttons may be less common now, but they can be found easily at flea markets and thrift stores for very little money. Start by amassing a large collection of old buttons to make these charming silhouette pieces of art.

HOW-TO: All you need to do is paint a prestretched artist canvas with flat, black paint and sketch out a design using white chalk. ➔ Then glue each button (using white craft glue) on top until the entire piece is covered.

Tarnished-Silver-Tray Table

SUPPLIES: Wooden table; screwdriver; tarnished, silver-plated tray; wood glue or strong epoxy.

One of my favorite places to bring out-of-town guests is the Boat House in the historic town of Lambertville, New Jersey. Down an out-of-the-way alley, there's a small, but perfectly cozy, drinking hole filled with genuine antique nautical paintings, artifacts, and knickknacks cramming every available inch of space. It's methodical hoarding. One upcycling idea they've done so brilliantly is to take ornate, tarnished, silver-plated trays (the kind you may have gotten as a wedding gift that never gets used) and turn them into working tables.

HOW-TO: It couldn't be any easier. Find a thrift-store wooden table and unscrew the top. It helps to flip the table so the top of the table is flush with the floor and the legs are straight up in the air; look for the screws holding them to the tabletop and unscrew away. ➔ Place the tray on top of the table legs, and secure it in place with a wood glue or strong epoxy; allow it to dry completely before using.

O'Keeffe
Viking

Floating Silk-Flower Arrangements

SUPPLIES: Silk flowers and watertight bowls and containers.

A collection of brightly colored silk flowers most likely won't fool anyone into thinking they're the real thing, but a single bud plucked from the grouping just might.

HOW-TO: Pluck the heads of the artificial flowers off their stems and leave the green leaves behind. ➔ Fill watertight bowls and containers with water, and float them individually as a centerpiece.

Cork-Tin-Can Organizers

SUPPLIES: Widemouthed tin cans (used for coffee, diced tomatoes, and quick-cooking oats); cork contact paper; photos, notes, or business cards; thumbtacks.

Widemouthed tin cans that once held coffee, diced tomatoes, and quick-cooking oats can be upcycled into desktop organizers.

HOW-TO: Wrap several layers of cork contact paper around each container; use smaller strips around the middle to add some interest in the overall design. ➔ Fill the containers with pens, pencils, paintbrushes, or whatever else you need organized but accessible. ➔ Decorate the fronts with photos, notes, or business cards; just thumbtack or pin them right to the fronts of the containers.

Glowing Rock-Salt Lights

SUPPLIES: Wooden or glass bowl, rock salt (available at Lowe's during the winter months; sold as de-icer), battery-powered string lights or light cord (I used the "Hemma" cord set from IKEA), an LED lightbulb, cordless drill outfitted with a 2-inch hole cutter drill bit, scissors.

There's something very ethereal about a glowing bowl of rock salt. It doesn't cast enough light to light up a room, but the soft glow of rock salt does add visual warmth and intrigue to whatever table you place the fixture on.

HOW-TO: For the wooden bowl, cut out a 2-inch hole along the side of the bowl, and run the light cord through the hole so the socket is snug inside against the edge. ➔ Screw in an LED lightbulb, and cover it with rock salt. ➔ For the glass bowl, place a battery-powered LED string light set on the bottom, turn on, and fill with salt.

Electronic-Cord Organizer

SUPPLIES: Wine corks, mini pipe clamp, extra large serving fork.

As a former decorating editor, one of my jobs whenever we were shooting a home for the pages of the magazine was to painstakingly use tape to hide cords from TVs and lamps so they wouldn't be in the finished photographs. Through the camera's lens, it was picture-perfect gorgeous; in reality, these rooms had roll after roll of gaffer's tape stuck to every piece of furniture running up and down the unseen sides of table and chair legs.

I'm one for believing if you have something plugged in, and the cord runs across the desk, accept the fact there's a cord and stop trying to deny it!

HOW-TO: Here, I took a collection of wine corks and bound them together using a mini pipe clamp from the hardware store. ➔ Then I simply jabbed an extra large serving fork (a junk-store find) and wrapped my iPhone cord around it like spaghetti—from iSore to iCute.

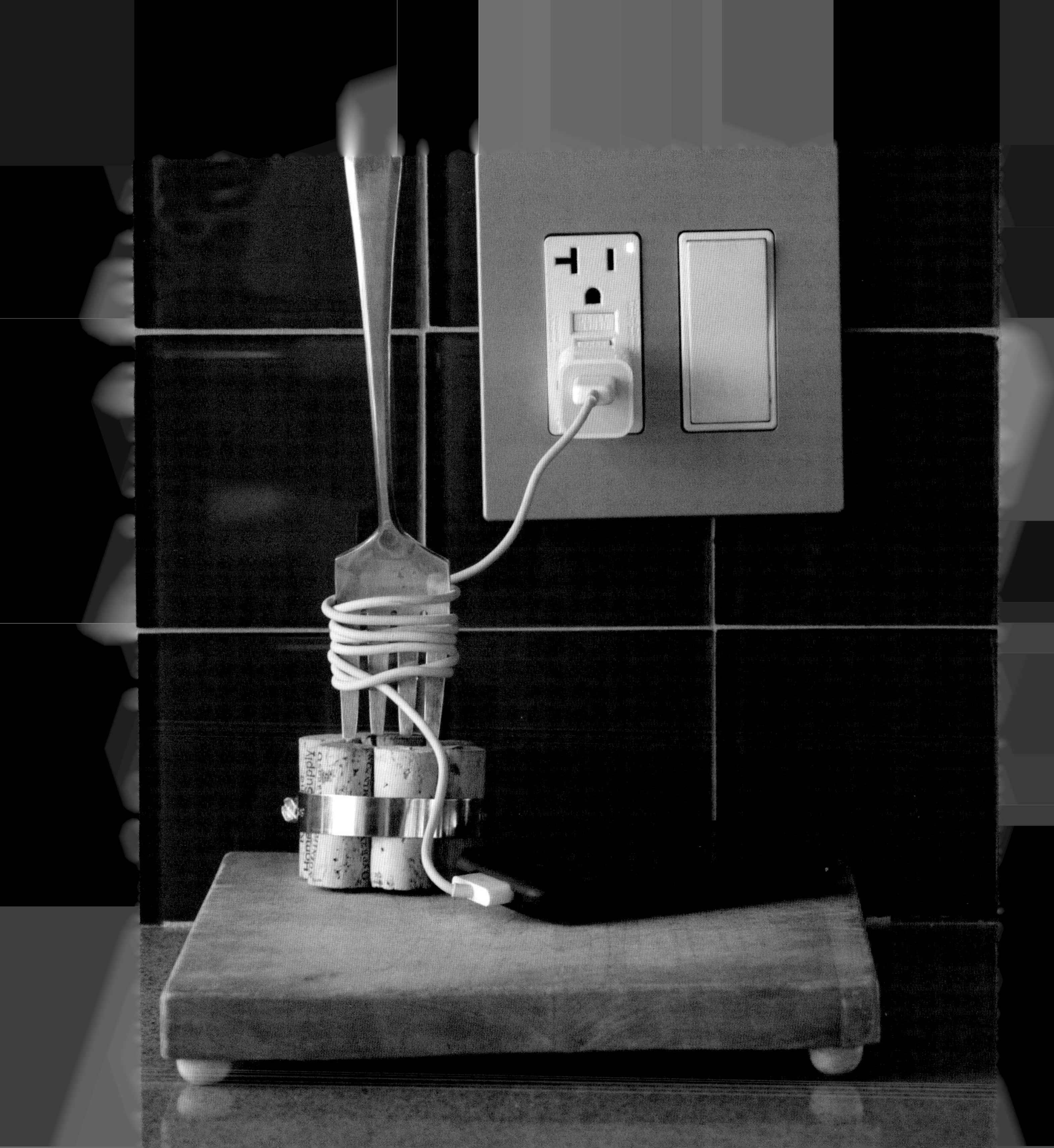

Zip-Tie Vines

SUPPLIES: Cords, zip ties, creamy white spray paint, faux-evergreen branch, scissors, white craft glue.

In almost any home office, you'll find endless cords connecting keyboards, monitors, wireless routers, and printers. Zip ties are an excellent way to keep them organized and to prevent tangling. One way to upcycle zip ties into something of more interest is to transform them into plastic vines.

HOW-TO: Just wrap the cords with zip ties about every 2 to 3 inches. ➔ Spray-paint a faux-evergreen branch (I got this at Michaels) a creamy white and allow it to dry. ➔ Snip pieces of the painted branch with scissors, and poke them into the zip-tie hole with a dab of glue.

Silk Garden Shop

Wallpaper-Swatch-Book Quilted Wall

SUPPLIES: Expired wallpaper swatch book and water.

Back when I was an editor at the now defunct *Country Home* magazine, my job was to constantly think of new ways to redefine country style. For many people, "country" conjures up images of Grandma's quilts, rusty weather vanes, and gingham tablecloths. But for me, it was an opportunity to draw influences from classic country design and evolve them to the twenty-first century.

One of my favorite projects involved taking a wallpaper swatch book—the wallcovering catalogs for consumers to flip through to see sheets of wallpaper samples—and use it to "quilt" a wall.

HOW-TO: This project is a cinch: secure an expired swatch book (ask the store for retired books before they throw them away), carefully remove each page without tearing, and attach the pieces to the wall. ➜ Since most wallpapers are already backed with glue that's activated with water, it can be just as easy to tear the pieces, dip them in water, and attach them to the wall.

CHAPTER TWO:

Upcycling Ideas for Entertaining

I once put together a kid's birthday party feature for a very big, influential parenting magazine. Here I am in New York City at their fancy offices in a meeting, discussing how we were going to "reinvent" children's birthday parties for a big magazine photo shoot. Imagine beautiful children deep inside a majestic redwood forest in California, playing with hand-glittered swords, enjoying cake and juice under whisper-thin silk tents, and going on treasure hunts by following a magical red string that meandered in between the giant evergreens. It sounded lovely, but the shoot ended up being an absolute production to the nth degree.

If you have a caravan of prop stylists, food stylists, child wranglers, event permits, catering, and a standby hotel where children close to having a meltdown could have a "time out," you too could throw this party. While the photos looked like a Ralph Lauren fantasy on steroids, it simply was not and will never be realistic for real parents to re-create.

I bring up this kid's birthday party because when it comes to entertaining in general, when the host works too hard to impress, it can lead to depress. A party isn't about showing off, but about great food, ample drinks, the right mix of friends or family and—this is the key—a host who is relaxed and having a great time. Nothing can be a bigger Debbie Downer at a party than a host who just can't chill out.

The great thing about these upcycling ideas for entertaining is that there's nothing here that's frivolous or holiday-specific. Whether you're throwing a birthday, housewarming, engagement, or casual dinner party, they'll work for any of these events. And don't think twice about having that cocktail before your guests arrive: drink it. It'll do a world of good.

Laminate-Countertop Grouted Tray

SUPPLIES: Unfinished wood tray, laminate-countertop chips, scissors, wood glue, powdered tile grout, bent knife, sponge, painter's tape, brush, craft paint.

I admit it, I'm a kitchen renovation-holic. I've renovated so many kitchens in my life you'd think I was addicted to picking out countertops, cabinets, and appliances. Not so and I'm not in denial: I just find myself renovating kitchens in my own home or at a client's house all the time.

Frequent renovations mean one thing: a huge collection of laminate-countertop sample chips. These little tiles are free at the home improvement store for homeowners to take home and compare in their kitchens. Since I tend to attract the indecisive client types, I have hundreds of them. And this project finally takes my odd collection and upcycles them into something I think is pretty darn cool.

HOW-TO: This is purely optional, but I highly recommend it: use scissors to snip off the edges of the countertop chips to make them appear to be chipped rock. ➔ Glue each piece onto the tray and allow them to dry until set. ➔ Mix the powdered grout in a bowl according to package instructions; spread the grout evenly over the chips, filling in the cracks. ➔ Wait twenty minutes and use a damp sponge to wipe off the excess grout. ➔ Dry it overnight. ➔ Place painter's tape on top of the grouted surface, and paint the entire tray in the color of your choice. ➔ Remove tape.

See finished project on p.101.

River-Rock-Handled Jar Mugs

SUPPLIES: Mason jar, E-6000 glue, two river rocks, painter's tape.

In the introduction for this book, I mentioned you would see a repeat of materials throughout the book, which might make you wonder if I wrote this entire thing over a weekend of mad crafting. I assure you, I did not. But I repeat certain materials because upcycling isn't a one-trick-pony-kind of a craft book. One crafting tool can be used almost a million different ways.

E-6000 glue is a smelly, probably hallucinogenic, glue that does wonders transforming two entirely separate materials into one. It is my upcycling secret weapon, and this project proves it makes the impossible, possible.

Mason jars are a common flea-market and thrift-store find. I love the raised glass words, colors, and widemouthed design of them. They are perfect to use for casual, summertime drinks.

HOW-TO: With E-6000 glue, you can attach smooth, long river rocks to the side of a mason jar to work as handles. ➔ Just squeeze a generous amount of glue to the side of the jar, stick the rock on top, and secure it in place with painter's tape. ➔ Dry it overnight, remove the tape, and tip back your favorite drink.

Hotel-Key-Card Breakfast-in-Bed Tray

SUPPLIES: Unfinished wood tray with collapsible legs, hotel key cards, white craft glue, powdered tile grout, bent knife, sponge, painter's tape, brush, craft paint.

As a bit of a road warrior, I accidentally amassed a collection of hotel key cards from all over the world. I'm not much of a collector, but these key cards just seem to accumulate, making their way into my wallet, my jean's back pocket, or languishing at the bottom of my carry-on suitcase. Over time, I would just toss these stowaways into a bowl in the bedroom until one day I realized I had a major collection.

Despite all the drawbacks of travel, there are perks: breakfast in bed. And what's a more memorable way to remember some of the best meals in bed than to upcycle these hotel key cards into a breakfast-in-bed tray. Now if I could just get someone to actually serve me breakfast in bed at home!

HOW-TO: Follow the same instructions for the Laminate-Countertop Grouted Tray (page 98), but instead use hotel key cards in place of the chips.

ACE HOTEL
NEW YORK
29TH AT
B'WAY
NH
Budapest
La Habana
RENAISSANCE HOTELS
www.nh-hotels.com
INSERT
W
HOTELS
ELITE
WELCOME
Marriott
REWARDS

Carpet-Sample Placemats

SUPPLIES: Twelve carpet-sample squares from the flooring department, roll of cork contact paper, scissors.

A friend of mine happens to be a public relations manager for a big-box home improvement store. I asked her, "Is it wrong that I go into your store and take handfuls of free samples to upcycle into something fun at home?" As I was saying this, I was imagining her texting her boss, "We need to call hotel store security and cue up some tapes." She advised that as long as I was visiting the store, familiarizing myself with their products, and hopefully buying something else, she had no problem with my minifreebie stash. Still, I have my doubts. So, may I make a suggestion? Patronize the store for your normal home improvement needs, and once in a while, take the freebies to upcycle.

HOW-TO: Cut a piece of cork contact paper slightly larger than the placemat. ➔ Remove the wax paper backing, and attach each square directly to the adhesive. ➔ Trim the excess cork with scissors.

Chinatown-Tote-Bag Floor Cushions

SUPPLIES: Styrofoam packing peanuts, large tote bags, scissors.

In the decorating chapter of this book, I shared a fun idea to upcycle nylon Chinatown shopping bags from extra large totes into a durable shower curtain. If that project didn't inspire you to stock up on totes, perhaps this one will: making floor cushions.

HOW-TO: In terms of difficulty, this project is as easy as they come. ➜ Collect Styrofoam packing peanuts—from deliveries, your neighbors, the office trash bin—and pack them tightly into the bags. ➜ Snip off the handles, sit on top, and relax.

Chinese-Food-Takeout-Chopstick Trivet

SUPPLIES: Chopsticks, hot glue gun, scissors.

I think one of the most common junk drawer staples is takeout food chopsticks. We all save them, but ultimately will probably never, ever use them.

Upcycling chopsticks into a handy trivet is a great example of form and function: the upcycled result looks like a wooden starburst, and your countertops will breathe a sigh of relief the next time you place a hot pot of stew on top. Your pricey Carrera marble countertop would thank you if it could.

HOW-TO: Glue four chopsticks into a square or five into a hexagon; it's all up to you on whatever design you want. ➔ Glue chopsticks on top of the base shape in a concentric circle, varying the lengths as you go along. You can really create whatever pattern you want. ➔ Once they're dry, use snips of smaller pieces of chopsticks to reinforce the entire trivet on the bottom by hot-gluing them into place.

Christmas-Light Hanging Pendant

SUPPLIES: Two identical grapevine wreaths and LED holiday strings lights.

One of the benefits of the Green Movement is that there are new technologies created that help our everyday lives be more efficient, safer, and sustainable. One of the best examples of this is the advent of LED—or Light Emitting Diodes—string lights that have replaced traditional incandescent bulb light strands. Instead of gobbling up tons of energy and burning out when one bulb expires, LED lights use a fraction of the energy. The bulbs don't shatter; they can last up to twenty-five years; and the light source doesn't get hot. If that wordy sentence just put you to sleep, let me *CliffsNotes* it for you: you can bundle these LED lights into giant balls of lights without the risk of it starting a fire.

HOW-TO: You can upcycle LED holiday strings lights in lots of different ways, and the design will mostly depend on the number of lights you have on hand. To make this extra large pendant light that I have hanging here on my back porch, just take two identical grapevine wreaths and squeeze one of them inside the other one at a 90 degree angle. ➜ Wrap the lights around the wreaths; hang the wreaths; and plug in the cord to illuminate. ➜ An easier way is to wrap the lights onto themselves, wrapping and wrapping until the ball of lights gets to the size you prefer.

Men's-Shirt Pennants

SUPPLIES: Variety of men's shirts, pinking shears, iron and ironing board, twine, Stitch Witchery tape.

In real life, I wear a men's size small (sometimes medium if I'm having what I call a Carb Fest Week), so you can imagine the looks I get when I shop for XXXL men's dress shirts at the local Goodwill store. I'm not shopping for clothes, but trying to get the maximum amount of upcycling fabric for my buck.

The classic patterns and colors of men's shirts are perfect for this festive upcycling project. Choose worn-out shirts that are destined for the donation bin or are torn and simply unrepairable.

HOW-TO: Cut large triangle pennants out of the shirts; keep the size of the pennants as consistent as possible. ➔ Place a pennant on the ironing board, and run a length of twine across the top and a length of Stitch Witchery tape along it. ➔ Fold the pennant over both pieces; place a hot iron on top, melting the tape; and create a loop for the twine to run inside. ➔ Repeat these steps and hang your pennants for a festive party.

Rubber-Dipped Utensils

SUPPLIES: Old silverware, binder clips, wire, can of plastic dip (available at any hardware store).

The imagination can run wild at a hardware store, and the possibilities alone in the paint department are endless. I bought a can of this plastic-dip material once with absolutely no idea what I could do with it. It was the beginning of October, and I started to decorate in anticipation for Halloween. I thought black dipped utensils using old silverware could give the pieces a fresh, autumnal look.

HOW-TO: Clip the ends of each utensil; run a piece of metal wire through the hook; and twist it around a steady surface (I used a metal rod that ran under an outdoor table) that lets each piece suspend in the air. ➔ Follow the plastic dip instructions, and slowly dip each handle into the container. Allow each dip to dry, and add additional dips until you get the desired effect. The drippier, and messier the coats, the better I think it looks. ➔ Dry the utensils overnight.

Flocked "Ceramic" Cans

SUPPLIES: Metal cans (used for coffee, beans, or tomatoes) and a can of wall texture spray.

This is a one-step upcycling project that looks more complicated than it really is. If you're in need of several modern-looking vases for a party, the best containers to use are those that are designed to be watertight.

HOW-TO: Start with metal cans that once held coffee, beans, tomatoes, or anything else you can rummage out of the recycling bin. Rinse them clean and pat dry. ➔ Use a can of wall texture spray (in the painting supply section at the home improvement store) and flock the cans following the instructions. It's as simple as that: insert the nozzle, press, and spray. ➔ Allow your vases to dry, fill them with water, and arrange your flowers.

Jar-Lid Dining Table

SUPPLIES: Metal grate table, clean jar lids, liquid nails adhesive.

Before

Las Vegas seems like the last place to find inspiration for a green crafting book, but Sin City ended up being a fruitful source for heavenly ideas. At the Barney's New York store, I spied a table that was made entirely out of jar lids, each one hand-welded to an individual metal rod and each of those metal rods bent, twisted, and forged together to create the base of the table. For years, I saved digital shots of this table on my computer's desktop, but realized there was no easy way I could ever make this table short of taking an apprenticeship at a blacksmith shop.

But I kept collecting jar lids nevertheless, out of my own recycling bin, from my neighbors and from the local sandwich shop that went through tons of them, from pickle to pepper jars. And one day, I looked through the windows at my metal grate outdoor table, then looked at the giant box of lids, and had an epiphany: I found my easy way to make a jar-lid table.

HOW-TO: Place clean lids all over the top of a metal grate table; it's important that it's grated so crumbs and spills can easily fall through for easy cleanup instead of being stuck in tiny crevices. ➔ Use liquid nails adhesive to adhere each jar lid to the table and allow them to dry. That's it.

Mini-Liquor-Bottle Bud Vase Collection

SUPPLIES: Variety of mini glass liquor bottles, fabric "puffy" paint, cream-colored flat spray paint, hot glue gun.

In addition to writing books, penning a newspaper column, hosting TV shows, and working with my celebrity clients, I also wear the ubiquitous "consultant" hat. One company I worked with is a boutique hotel chain that I helped make green from the inside/out. One of the many items they often found intermixed in the trash (and not the in-room recycling bins) were the little glass liquor bottles. I always thought these miniaturized bottles of tequila, vodka, and scotch (and even the half-splits of bad Chardonnay) were adorable. Over time, as I spent time in my client's hotel rooms, I would ask the hotel housekeepers to fish out bottles for me so I could add them to my upcycling to-do list.

Anyway, if you travel a lot, here's a nice project to upcycle those little bottles into a bud vase. For those of you who don't drink or travel often, become friendly with your local hotel that has minibars in their rooms. If your request is met with a confused look, just show them this book and say "I want to make this."

HOW-TO: Hot-glue the bottles together on the side to create one, solid bud vase collection. ➔ Use the puffy paint to add texture and dimension—small dots running up and down or across or randomly scattered. ➔ Allow them to dry completely and then spray several coats of light spray paint.

Paint-Stirrer Lanterns

SUPPLIES: Glass cylindrical vase smaller in height than a paint stirrer (I save them whenever people send me flowers; also available at Michaels craft stores), paint stirrers, two metal pipe clamps (I used 12-inch round ones), flathead screwdriver, pillar candle.

Sometimes the simplicity of the material and shape of the items being upcycled really shines when they're grouped together. These paint-stirrer lanterns look great when left raw, but could also look very Jackson Pollock–inspired when using actual used stirrers that you've used to mix paint cans. While attempting to amass a collection of used stirrers, it might be a good idea to become friendly with a neighborhood professional painter. I'm sure he'll be confused as why in the heck you would want them, but at least he knows they're going to be reused instead of being tossed out.

HOW-TO: Loosen both pipe clamps so it fits loosely around the vase. ➔ Arrange paint stirrers around the vase, and tighten the clamps as you add stirrers; continue until the entire vase is covered, and tighten the clamps until they are securely in place. ➔ Light a pillar candle and place it inside. Remember to never leave a lit candle unattended.

Patrón-Tequila Oil Lights

SUPPLIES: Patrón bottle, funnel, lamp oil, ¾-inch fiberglass wick, scissors, 1½-inch washer with a ½-inch opening.

One night in Los Angeles, I was working with a celebrity client over dinner and she finally blurted out, "What on earth do you keep looking at?" Apparently I was drifting and not making any eye contact with her: I was staring at a Patrón bottle at the bar. I was obsessed with the organic shape of the bottle and figuring out a cool way to upcycle it. My starlet dinner date shared my crafting dilemma, and there we sat, together, looking at a bottle of tequila and pondering how to upcycle it. Then it occurred to me: fill it with lamp oil and a wick to make outdoor lanterns.

HOW-TO: This project is almost too easy: use a funnel to fill the Patrón bottle with about 3 inches of lamp oil; add a ¾-inch fiberglass wick inside; and trim so it's ½ inch above the opening of the bottle. ➔ Secure it in place by running it through a 1½-inch washer with a ½-inch opening, and rest the washer on top of the bottle. ➔ Light your lantern, and throw a party. As always, never leave an open flame unattended. Also, make sure the wick continues to be exposed ½-inch above the washer, or it may become a fire hazard.

PATRÓN

Potato-Chip-Bag "Silver Leafed" Mirror

SUPPLIES: A square piece of wood, 4 or 5 potato or pita chip bags with a shiny Mylar-like interior, soap/water, scissors, spray adhesive, X-Acto knife, square template.

A part of me wonders if this project would have come to fruition had I been on the Atkins diet. When I eat potato chips, I like to make sure every last chip gets devoured, and I often catch my reflection when I poke my head inside the bag. (Really!) And Voilà: there is my inspiration for the potato-chip-bag mirror.

If you've read my previous books, you know I've used chip bags to gift wrap presents. But upcycling means one material can have a million different uses, and this mirror is no exception. While you may not be able to see a 20/20 reflection of yourself in this mirror, it does resemble a true silver-leafed mirror you might see in an antique store.

HOW-TO: Have a carb fest and eat chips like a competitive food eater. ➜ Rinse out the chip bags with soap and water so the interior isn't greasy. ➜ Cut the bag open with scissors so it's one flat piece. ➜ With an X-Acto knife, use a template to cut out squares of material (I used a plastic jewel case from a CD). ➜ Cover a piece of wood with spray adhesive, and add each square of bag material—shiny side out—to the piece of wood. ➜ Use it as a tray or hang it above a bar using a hook, rope, and nails.

Frosted-"Cookie" Cookbook Weight

SUPPLIES: Flat rock, white Pébéo Porcelaine glaze, glass beads.

I love to cook, and I love cookbooks. As a child, my brother would head to the science-fiction section of the bookstore, my sister would be wherever those Adventures in Babysitting books were, and I'd be in the cookbook aisle poring over every single book.

Today, I have amassed a pretty large cookbook collection that is splattered, worn, and well-loved. And I have this to say to the publishers of these books: why can't you publish them so they stay opened to the page I'm working from?

If you're a foodie or know someone who is, this is a fun, useful item to make for them to live with their cookbook collection. The "frosted" rocks help weigh down the pages, and they really do look like a sweet treat right out of the kitchen.

HOW-TO: Find a nice, flat rock in your backyard or on a walk through the woods. ➔ Scrub it clean. ➔ Pour white Pébéo Porcelaine glaze on top, and let it drip along the sides like frosting. ➔ Shake glass beads on top to mimic sprinkles. ➔ Set it aside to dry for twenty-four hours.

Salt cod à la bénédictine

Tiered Trays

SUPPLIES: Mismatched glass, metal, or ceramic plates and cups, E-6000 glue, painter's tape.

Mismatched or chipped plates and cups are something most people have in their kitchen cabinets. They are also the least expensive thing you can find at flea markets and yard sales. This upcycling project celebrates the individual design and worn look of these pieces by marrying them together into impressive tiered trays.

The key to this project is the glue: E-6000. Surprised? For those of you who are flipping through the book instead of reading project to project, let me reiterate: it is an incredibly strong adhesive that will bond the pieces together so securely you can pick up the entire tiered tray with your fingertips without fear of it falling apart.

HOW-TO: The overall tiered trays look best when you stack pieces that are from the same family of material: glass, ceramic, or metal. Place the largest plate on the bottom, and choose a cup to place in the middle; glue it in place by squeezing a generous amount of E-6000 glue on the bottom of the cup. Be sure to work in a well-ventilated place, since the glue is rather smelly. ➜ Choose another plate to place on top of the cup, and secure it in place by squeezing more glue onto the rim of the cup. ➜ Repeat these steps until you finish the tray. ➜ Secure everything in place by wrapping painter's tape all around the tray, and allow it to dry for twenty-four hours before using. ➜ If you want to wash the trays, be sure to hand wash them and dry them with a clean towel.

CHAPTER THREE:

Upcycling Ideas for Giving

I'm a big believer that when it comes to giving gifts, it really, truly is the thought that counts. People often confuse thoughtfulness with thriftiness, which really isn't the case. For example, if someone has been coveting a Hermes Birkin bag for decades and was surprised when you gave them one for their birthday, it shows you've listened and helped turn their dream gift into a reality (and you probably had to refinance your house, but let's leave that to Suze Orman to dissect, shall we?). On the other hand, an economical, thoughtful gift could be doing everything on their weekend to-do list: mowing the lawn, raking leaves, and taking out the trash. Free time in anyone's hectic lives is a precious commodity.

Gifts that are handmade are perfect for all sorts of gift-giving situations. I use the term "handmade" loosely here. Not everything that's handmade has to involve crocheting, baking, staining, or monogramming. These are projects that you can have in your upcycling repertoire when, say, you totally forget it's your best friend's birthday. And they also involve permission to go use store-bought items that you embellish yourself to make it look less last-minute and more thoughtful.

Book Vases

SUPPLIES: A hardcover book, manila folder, scissors, pencil or marker, X-Acto knife, white craft glue.

True book lovers may want to look away or completely disregard this project because this one involves taking the written word and trashing it. Don't use a first edition of Steinbeck's *The Grapes of Wrath* to make one of these, but instead raid your bookshelf for hardcover trashy novels you won't miss after you've upcycled them. If you haven't got a single book to spare, your local Goodwill store usually has a plethora of books that have been donated and are sold for a tiny fraction of the cost.

HOW-TO: Cut the manila folder in half so there's just one flat piece. ➔ Lay the one piece on top of an open book, and trim the excess paper away from the folder on the top and bottom. ➔ Draw a silhouette of a vase with a pencil or marker on the folder, and cut it out with scissors; cut that shape in half and use it as a template to cut out pages inside the book. ➔ Hold the template flush against the binding of the book, and use the X-Acto knife to carefully cut out the shape several pages at a time. ➔ When you've cut all the pages, carefully remove the book's hardcover jacket and fold the book accordion style so the front and back pages meet to create a 3-D vase. ➔ Glue in place and display.

by
JOHN H. STOKE
Eighth Printing

String Scented Diffusers

SUPPLIES: Small, empty glass bottles (Pellegrino, salad dressing, and other short bottles), white craft glue, natural twine/string, diffuser oil, Chinese-food-takeout chop

Using refills is a great way to save money and cut down on wasteful packaging. This project takes advantage of the fact you can buy little jars of essential oils for reed diffusers instead of buying the whole kit. By upcycling old jars and chopsticks, you can make a DIY diffuser that in my opinion looks better than any store-bought diffuser.

HOW-TO: Work in three sections at a time: the top, middle, and bottom of the bottle. Cover the top third with white craft glue, and begin wrapping the string or twine around the bottle. ➔ Press the string firmly into the glue, and hold until it is set in place. ➔ Continue wrapping around and around until the entire bottle is covered. ➔ Fill the bottle with diffuser oil, and place chopsticks inside to help absorb the oil and diffuse the fragrance into the air.

Button Monogrammed Journals

SUPPLIES: Photo album, journal, or storage box; piece of chalk; buttons; white craft glue.

Inexpensive and colorful photo albums, journals, and storage boxes can be found at discount stores for very little money. One way to customize them for gift giving is to use the initials of the gift recipient.

HOW-TO: Use a piece of chalk to sketch out the initials on the front, and glue buttons inside the chalk lines using craft glue.

Upcycled Cashmere Sweater Accessories

SUPPLIES: Cashmere sweater (including turtleneck), scissors, hot water bottle, safety pin, plastic-cuff bracelets, hot glue gun, eye mask, fabric glue.

It's hard to give away, let alone donate a cashmere sweater when you get a hole in it. Sure, you can't wear it, but it's just impossible to part with such a pricey purchase. Cashmere is expensive and prized, but when it's worn out, you can give it a second luxurious life in the form of beautiful accessories that can be used and loved every day.

HOW-TO:

Cuffs: Snip them off to use as a reusable coffee sleeve for your morning coffee. When you forget to bring a reusable thermos, you can save a little paper by choosing not to use the cardboard sleeve when sipping your nonfat, soy latte.

Turtleneck Sweaters: Use the top half to cover a hot water bottle. Just snip the top third of a cashmere sweater turtleneck, and cover a hot water bottle; secure the material in place with a safety pin in the back.

Remnant Sweater Fabric: Upcycle plastic-cuff bracelets by hot-gluing sweater fabric all over the outside; you'll feel the soft and cozy cashmere sweater on your wrists instead of clunky, cold plastic.

Or, cover an existing eye mask with fabric. Cut pieces that match the front and back of the eye mask, and use fabric glue to adhere it in place. Use two strips of cashmere fabric to cover the straps for extra coziness.

Keyboard Journals

SUPPLIES: Old, broken computer keyboard, journal, flathead screwdriver, hot glue gun.

If I had to choose one thing that I bet is stashed away in the back of everyone's closet in their home office, it's an old, broken computer keyboard. We have no idea why or who would ever want to use it again, but we just can't bring ourselves to get rid of it. Well, it's time to pull it out and upcycle the alphabetic keys for this adorable project.

HOW-TO: Use a flathead screwdriver to remove the keys off the keyboard. Once you remove a few, you should be able to use your fingers to remove the rest. ➔ Using a hot glue gun, glue the keys to the front of a journal to either completely cover the surface or decorate just a section of it. ➔ Spell out names, cute phrases, or just use a randomly selected grouping of keys to decorate.

A P R I L
A L B U M →

Concrete Water Bottles

SUPPLIES: Plastic water or soda bottle, quick-drying concrete, paint stirrer, plastic funnel, X-Acto knife.

The plastic water bottle has become the nemesis of the environmental movement. It represents everything against sustainability: a nonrenewable, petroleum-based package; a natural product that is abundant and unnecessarily bottled; and an outright superfluous item that millions of consumers toss out on a daily basis.

Even if you've made the pledge to stop drinking bottled water, you can't escape the overflowing trash cans full of them at the subway platform, gym, or office. One project I love to do is to upcycle the actual containers and turn them into concrete bottles (which can serve as cool doorstops) in just one easy step. When you're done making this project, you can still toss the old plastic bottle into the recycling bin.

HOW-TO: Start by adding double the amount of water as instructed on a container of quick-drying concrete; you can pick up a container at any home improvement store like Lowe's. ➔ Mix the concrete mixture with a stirrer (I use a paint stirrer) for a few minutes until it's smooth and lump-free. ➔ Place a plastic funnel on top of the water or soda bottle, and pour the concrete mixture into the bottle until it has reached the top. ➔ Wait a few seconds, and tap the bottle against the table to release any air bubbles and help it settle. ➔ Add more concrete until it's completely full. ➔ Dry it overnight. ➔ Score the bottom of the plastic bottle with an X-Acto knife, and peel away the plastic.

Sweater-Dryer Balls

SUPPLIES: Tennis balls, old sweater material, safety pins.

Ironing seems to be the most dreaded of all household chores. One way to cut back is to fluff laundry as it dries. Homekeeping experts have long advised adding tennis balls to the dryer to fluff sheets, towels, and shirts; the tennis balls agitate clothes and reduce clumping and wrinkling, also helping them to dry faster and more evenly. But if you don't monitor the drying time carefully, the faint smell of burnt rubber can easily perfume your clothes.

HOW-TO: An easy way to prevent that is to simply wrap the tennis balls in old sweater material, twist the excess into a knot, and close it with a safety pin. The layer of argyle or L.L.Bean woolen will create just enough of a soft barrier to prevent the burnt rubber smell and help cut back on unnecessary ironing. This is a great housewarming gift that can be added to a wicker basket full of eco-friendly laundry detergent.

Wilson
US OPEN

CD Dumbbells

SUPPLIES: 12-inch threaded rod, ¼-inch in diameter (from the hardware store), four matching bolts, approximately 100 CDs.

Since I founded an environmental group in my teenage years, I often get invited to come speak to high school students about activism and sustainability. These visits remind me of two things: #1) how optimistic I was as a teenager and #2) how old I've become. I tell tales of how we didn't have Internet access when I was a freshman in high school and how America Online used to send out millions of compact discs in the mail to tempt consumers to try their downloadable software for dial-up service. The looks of pure confusion I get from teenagers today make me realize I lose them at the words "dial-up."

But if you're around my age, you may recall the mailbox full of these junk-mail AOL discs. And it was these CDs that inspired me to think of a functional and beautiful way to upcycle them: CD Dumbbells. Soft to the touch and oh-so modern-looking, each dumbbell weighs about seven pounds. Too light for a strenuous workout, but just right for some added resistance when doing crunches. Is it going to replace the need for a gym? Hardly. But they are fun to make and could be useful to some. For the father or tech-savvy person who is impossible to find a gift for, this handmade gift is a semi-gag gift that's perfect for them.

HOW-TO: Thread one bolt from each end approximately 4 inches in. ➔ Thread 50 CDs on each end up to the bolts, and secure them in place at each end of the rod with another bolt.

Newspaper Fire Logs

SUPPLIES: Lots of newspaper, a broomstick, a sink full of water, eucalyptus (optional fragrance).

Only in America would we find a way to manufacture firewood into a mass-produced product: Duraflame logs. Why not try making your own fake firewood? If you're heading to a holiday party during a chilly, winter night, a basket full of these is a great gift to bring to warm the hearth at their festivities.

HOW-TO: Start by soaking newspaper in the sink. ➔ Wrap sections of wet paper around a broomstick over and over until you achieve a thickness that resembles a piece of firewood. ➔ Press it all together, and squeeze out the excess water. ➔ The broomstick will pull right out and leave you with a wet newspaper log; place in a warm, sunny spot so it dries out completely; this could take a week. ➔ For extra aromatherapy scent, stuff the middle hole with dried eucalyptus to add fragrance to the fireplace when it burns.

Hotel Soap on a Rope

SUPPLIES: This is one very cheap project to make: all you need is lots of hotel soap, nylon rope, and a cordless drill outfitted with a ½-inch drill bit.

One thing I'm guilty of is that I love to stash all the free mini bottles of shampoo, conditioner, and soap that come in hotel rooms. Since I'm a bit of a road warrior and less of a hoarding worrier, I've amassed quite a collection of toiletries over the year that I intend to actually use. One fun project is to take that collection of different shaped and colored minibars of soap and make a "jeweled" necklace of sorts from it. It's a fun gift for the laziest person you might know: all they have to do is wear the soap necklace, stand in the shower, and let gravity do its job.

HOW-TO: Just drill a hole through each piece of soap—the middle or at the ends—and thread them through the rope. ➔ Tie a knot at the ends—and voilà!—hotel soap on a rope.

Sock-Shoe Forms

SUPPLIES: Cotton ankle socks, large safety pins, polyester pillow, small ribbon (optional).

It makes sense that if you want to preserve the shape of a shoe, instead of pricey wooden shoe forms, use old socks instead. This upcycling project uses ankle length sports socks, but any thick, cotton sock will do. If you're planning to make these for yourself, use old socks. But if you want to make some as gifts for friends, think brand new. Again, upcycling isn't just about transforming trash, but turning inexpensive finds into something better; why not turn dollar-store socks into charming shoe forms?

HOW-TO: Rip open an old pillow, and use the polyester fill on the inside. ➔ Fill a sock with tightly packed polyester fill; fold down the edges of the sock inward; and use a large safety pin to secure the opening closed. ➔ Tie a small ribbon for adornment to the safety pin.

Spare-Change Catchall Tray

SUPPLIES: Terra-cotta saucer, mosaic grout, frosting knife, hot glue gun, sponge, pennies.

As a magazine home decorating editor, I've seen the good, the bad, and the bizarre come across my desk. At a decorating trade show, I once saw an area rug made entirely out of hundreds of one-dollar bills all intricately knit together. I thought it was the craziest idea ever and wondered why anyone would want to literally decorate their home with currency.

Well, never say never because I love this easy upcycling idea to turn—wait for it—spare change into a catchall bowl.

HOW-TO: Glue the pennies to the bottom of the terra-cotta saucer. ➔ Cover the entire surface with a thin layer of grout with the frosting knife and dry according to package instructions. ➔ Approximately twenty minutes later, wipe off the excess grout with a damp sponge. ➔ Allow it to dry overnight before using.

ALTOIDS
smalls
SUGAR-FREE
CINNAMON
50 MINTS
TAKE-OUT **TOTAL
CHANGE DUE$
Approval No: 589090
Card Issuer: AMEX
Amount: $13.35
EMTEK

Soda-Can Sequined Tote Bag

SUPPLIES: Soda cans, 1-inch hole punch, scissors, brad punch, tote bag.

If I had to choose one type of genre that I love to watch at the movie theater, that answer would easily be documentaries. I love to see brilliant artists, designers, activists, and others doing what they do best and see their entire creative and work process truly documented. When I was a teenager, the designer Isaac Mizrahi had a documentary called *Unzipped* that showed the entire process it took to create a fashion collection: from inspiration to sketches to creation to the final fashion show presentation.

In his fashion collection, he had taken Coca-Cola and 7UP cans and punched them out into sequins that were used in skirts and gowns. The end result was an eco-chic creation that showed that environmentally friendly fashion could be fun, colorful, and—this is key—oh so stylish. This project pays homage to Isaac and his quirky upcycling idea.

HOW-TO: Cut the top and bottom off the soda can, and snip a straight line down the can using regular sharp scissors to make one flat piece of aluminum. ➜ Wipe clean. ➜ Use the 1-inch hole punch to punch out circles of aluminum sequins. ➜ Use a brad punch, and follow the instructions to attach each sequin to the front of the tote bag. ➜ Create whatever pattern or combination of colors you want for your design.

Setaro
PASTA DI SEMOLA DI GRANO DURO
Trafila in bronzo
LA VALLE
San Marzano
POMODORI PELATI ITALIANI
PEELED
D.O.P.
DOUBLE ACTING
NET WT. 10 OZ.
Nutrition Facts
7.5 FL OZ (222 mL)
680 g

Valentine's Day Love Bottle

SUPPLIES: Glass soda or liquor bottle or a widemouthed glass jar; colorful sand or glitter; fabric (for cut-out hearts); florist wire; glue.

Like a message in a bottle, here's a way to express your feelings of love to someone else for Valentine's Day or anytime you're feeling romantic. This could also be an adorable project to do with kids on a rainy day.

HOW-TO: Fill a bottle—a glass soda or liquor bottle or a widemouthed glass jar—with colorful sand, glitter, hand-cut hearts, or anything else that you think will look and feel romantic. Colorful sand can be found in the floral department at any Michaels craft store. ➔ Use a piece of florist wire, and poke it into the bottle's cork or tape it in the middle of the jar lid. ➔ Glue fabric hearts along the wire, and insert the wire inside the jar to create the illusion of floating hearts.

Wood-Grain Journals

SUPPLIES: One or two pieces of PVC flooring samples, scissors, hole punch, string or binder clips, journal or appointment calendar refill paper.

One of the very first upcycling projects I've ever done is still with me today, testament that handmade can also mean long-lasting. But it could be the fact I used indestructible PVC faux-wood flooring material to make my everyday Filofax appointment book.

PVC may not be a very eco-friendly choice to cover the floors in your home, but in these very small quantities, it can be a safe material to use as the cover for an everyday journal that will never dull, fade, or tear. You can find free samples in the flooring department in all sorts of different patterns and colors. I happen to like the wood-grain style because it's kitschy, but use whatever color or pattern you desire.

HOW-TO: Cut the PVC samples to size according to the size of paper refills; either use two exact pieces of flooring samples or bend one large piece to make one full cover. ➜ Use the existing holes in the refill paper as guides to punch out holes along the edge of the tile samples. ➜ Use binder clips or string to bind it all together.

Scrap-Wood Postcard

SUPPLIES: Wood pieces about the size of a standard postcard (about 6 × 4 inches); handsaw (to trim down larger pieces); sandpaper (to smooth down the edges); rubber stamps or a Phillips head screwdriver (to scratch directly into the wood).

In any home improvement store with a lumber section, there is a wood-cutting station where customers can trim down all types of wood to meet their DIY needs. In the trash can, you'll find all sorts of throwaway scraps that are perfect for this project.

HOW-TO: To decorate the postcard, you can use stamps available at the craft store or a Phillips head screwdriver to scratch directly into the wood. Use the appropriate amount of postage to send your love card in the mail.

POSTCARD
HAVING A
GREAT TIME!!
MISS YOU!
For
Date
Place
RSVP
P
O
S
T
C
A
R
D

IRVING FARM
COFFEE COMPANY
www.IrvingFarm.com
CAUTION: HOT BEVERAGE

CHAPTER FOUR:

Upcycling Ideas for Kids

(and Those Young at Heart)

One of my earliest memories involves my family packing up the station wagon and going on long road trips to resorts or warm beach excursions. For me, it was never really about the final destination, but the journey in getting there. Our family had one of those cars where the third row in the station wagon faced outward toward the car behind us, otherwise jokingly known as "the carbon monoxide" seat. This was my seat. And the night before any summer vacation trip, I would grab a roll of paper towels, Windex, and the DustBuster vacuum and clean up just my area of the car. It actually made me happy to see a very distinct line between clean and dirty, a line that separated myself from my siblings and made it clear to them: cross this and you've crossed too far. Once cleaned, I'd bring in a variety of coloring books, toys, and collectible cars that would entertain me on my trip and create a mini-playroom of sorts for myself. Yes, even at this young age, I was styling the backseat of my family's Oldsmobile station wagon.

On one, extremely hot summer day, as we crossed the border into South Carolina and dined at a roadside attraction called South of the Border, I left my crayons inside the car. Two hours later, I returned to a puddle of melted crayons that swirled together into one big mess. But instead of having a meltdown over melted crayons, I was fascinated by the color combinations and let the air-conditioning chill the mess into new crayons. When I drew with the swirled pieces, I got new color combinations and swirls all over the paper.

This was proof to me that recycling could be fun. And your kids can learn this too. Instead of sorting recyclables from the trash into special bins where a big truck takes it away to some magical land, your kids can actually see something transform right in front of their eyes. From collecting the materials to helping with the project to seeing the final product come to life, they learn lessons in resourcefulness when upcycling with you. Instead of learning that something useless should be thrown "away," here they can use their imagination to envision it as something else.

3-D Globes

SUPPLIES: Desktop globe; E-6000 glue; painter's tape (optional); miniature trees, animals, and memorabilia (like a miniature Eiffel Tower or Statue of Liberty) to place all over the globe. Gift shops, toy stores, and eBay are great places to find these things.

It's slightly sad that in the age of Google maps, GPS systems, and navigation tools that can pinpoint your exact location at any given time, globes are becoming obsolete. I remember growing up with a desktop globe as a child, and I'd spin it as fast as I could with my sister, close my eyes, and stop it with my finger. Wherever my finger landed was where I was going to travel when I grew up.

Many people have these globes stashed away in the attic. This fun project teaches children where certain animals or landmarks are all over the world.

HOW-TO: Use E-6000 glue to adhere the miniature objects all over the globe's surface; if you want to glue something that will dry upside down, just tape the object in place with painter's tape and remove the tape when the object is dry.

You can also twist a cardboard globe in half at the equator; it'll pry apart easily with a dull knife. Just use a store-bought light cord (the kind you plug in and has a socket at the end) and run it inside one of the globe halves. You'll need to cut a hole at the top of the globe that is large enough to fit the plug through, but small enough to keep the socket inside from slipping through; I used a 2-inch drill bit on a cordless drill to make this one.

Found Alphabet Art

SUPPLIES: Decorations for alphabet, hot glue gun, store-bought shadow box.

Make this a fun scavenger hunt for the kids: they have to raid junk drawers, desks, backpacks, and any other place where random junk may be lurking to create a shadow-box alphabet. Be creative: use puffy paint to spell out a letter, a stray Scrabble piece, twist wire into whatever consonant or vowel you need. The more random and colorful, the better it looks.

HOW-TO: Use a hot glue gun to attach your alphabet inside a store-bought shadow box.

PUT-A-PENNY COIN

Coffee-Sleeve Crowns

SUPPLIES: Paper coffee sleeves, white craft glue, scissors, decorations (glitter, stickers, paint).

Whenever I forget to bring my reusable thermos to the coffee house for my morning fix, I feel guilty. So, I forgo the plastic lid and paper sleeve and do a balancing act of switching the scalding hot cup between hands as I take baby sips without spilling. And for those of you wondering why I just don't forgo coffee altogether clearly do not understand that not having my coffee fix in the morning is not an option.

If you prefer not to have third-degree burns on the palms of your hands, the cardboard sleeves can be collected and upcycled into paper crowns. On my desk at home, I have single sleeve crowns that simply adorn my desk. But for kids (and maybe if you feel rather princely one day), you can combine several sleeves to fit around the head to regally wear.

HOW-TO: To make a single crown, snip the top of the sleeve with sharp scissors to cut out interesting shapes and decorate it however you want. ✦ To make a wearable crown, rip open the sleeves and glue several of them together until it's long enough to fit comfortably around the head and decorate. ✦ Allow the glue to dry completely before wearing.

IRVING FARM
COFFEE COMPANY
www.IrvingFarm.com
CAUTION: HOT BEVERAGE

Crayon Vases

SUPPLIES: Variety of crayons with paper sleeves removed, old Pyrex measuring cups no longer used for cooking, an old cooking pot.

This upcycling project came to life by accident one night when I was melting crayons over a double boiler in the kitchen in preparation for an appearance the next morning on *Today* to show Hoda Kotb and Kathie Lee Gifford how to recycle crayons. With some excess melted wax at the bottom of the Pyrex container, I decided to let it cool. What popped out was a shiny, swirly, beautiful creation that I realized could be made into the most amazing upcycled crayon vases.

HOW-TO: Bring around two inches of water to a simmering boil on the stove. ➔ Break up the crayons into small pieces, and place them inside the Pyrex measuring cup, about two to three inches inside the cup. ➔ Place the measuring cup inside the pot, and slowly heat the crayons until completely melted. ➔ Remove the Pyrex container from the pot, and allow it to cool for one minute. Using a dry dishtowel, hold the Pyrex container by the handle, and slowly swirl it, coating the sides of the cup with thin layers of melted crayon. Keep swirling until the entire inside is coated and there is no more melted wax pooled at the bottom of the cup. ➔ Place the cup in the freezer for one hour. ➔ To remove the vase, press your fingers on the inside of the vase against the glass until it releases; it should pop out easily.

Crayola

Furniture Stag Heads

SUPPLIES: Legs from chairs and small tables, small handsaw, wood screws, cordless screwdriver, buttons, spoons and forks, hot glue gun, wood plaque (from Michaels craft stores), acrylic paint and brush.

Originally, this project was supposed to use your child's old stuffed toys that you'd decapitate, mount onto wood, and display in their bedroom as faux-stag heads. Keep in mind, this is a project idea coming from a guy who doesn't have kids. . . . Some of my friends pulled me aside and gently pointed out that taking your child's treasured toy and mounting it to the wall might be perceived as insensitive.

So, we rethought the project and thankfully came up with something that I think is much better and creative.

HOW-TO: Paint the wood plaques a solid color and allow them to dry. ➔ Shop flea markets and thrift stores for old chairs and small tables; look for incredibly inexpensive ones since you'll only be using the legs. ➔ Detach the legs and use a small handsaw to cut them down to size. ➔ Use one leg for the "face" or two matching legs as "antlers." Screw them into place from behind the plaque into the legs. ➔ Play around with spoons and forks to make horns and ears; bend, twist, or manipulate them with your hands to bring them to life. ➔ Use hot glue to attach them to the legs, and add a button for the nose.

Blown-Up Kid's Artwork

SUPPLIES: Your kid's original art (made into a full-color poster at a copy shop) and a frame.

A few years ago, I strolled into a fancy art gallery in New York City. It was one of those galleries that A: did not have prices readily available and B: had questionable artwork that I couldn't tell if it was actually art or, say, an emergency exit sign.

One piece I was drawn to resembled a toddler's drawing on yellow paper, blown up to epic proportions, and beautifully framed in a white shadow box. Since most parents think every doodle their child makes is pure genius, I thought this was a nice idea of upcycling some of your kid's very best artwork.

HOW-TO: All you have to do is bring your original art to any FedEx office or copy shop and ask to have it blown up to a full-color poster. Then frame your poster and display it.

Kid's-T-shirt Artwork

SUPPLIES: Kid's T-shirt, artist stretcher wooden bars (from a craft store), staple gun, scissors.

Is it just me or is kid's clothing just getting cuter and cuter each season? It's sad when they can no longer fit into an itty-bitty T-shirt, but not every piece needs to be relegated to the Goodwill donation box. Turn a few of your favorite tees into kid's-T-shirt artwork.

HOW-TO: It's simple: pick up artist stretcher wooden bars at the craft store and assemble them together into a square. ➔ Stretch the T-shirt over it, flip it over, and staple gun the shirt into place. As you staple each side to the bars, pull the shirt so it's taut over the frame. ➔ Trim the excess fabric away with scissors and display.

EXPLORE
WHAT YOU
FIND...
abcd
fgh jk
lmn p
qrst
vwxyz.
CUB SCOUT DAY CAMP
CUB
SCOUT
INVESTIGATOR
CRADLE OF LIBERTY COUNCIL

Lego Journals

SUPPLIES: Cordless drill outfitted with ¼-inch drill bit; journal refill paper; flat, landscape-style Lego pieces; string with needle; small Lego pieces to decorate with, hot glue gun (optional).

Even as children become technologically savvy, it's heartwarming to know the popularity of Legos continues to thrive with each generation. Stray Lego pieces can be upcycled into these fun and colorful journals in just a few simple steps. While a parent is needed to operate the cordless drill, the child can adorn the front with whatever Lego decoration their heart desires.

HOW-TO: Choose two large, flat pieces of Legos (the kind that are bases for most Lego projects) that are about the same size of the dimensions of the inside of the journal. ➔ Use a cordless drill to make holes along the edges of both Lego pieces to match up with the prepunched holes in the paper. ➔ Stitch them together using string and a needle. ➔ Decorate the front. ➔ Tip: If you want the front decoration pieces to be permanent, use a little bit of hot glue when attaching them.

2011

Lipstick-Case Crayons

SUPPLIES: Old crayons; Pyrex container; double boiler; clean, empty lipstick cases.

My young niece cannot wait to wear makeup and begs me relentlessly to let her try on nail polish or lipstick whenever we're shopping at a department store. She's not old enough for kindergarten, but she already knows *rouge* is her color.

While I would never allow her to wear makeup, I think these upcycled lipstick-case crayons are a fair compromise to satisfy her needs while making sure she doesn't grow up too fast.

HOW-TO: To make these, melt old crayons in a Pyrex container over a double boiler of simmering water. ➔ Pour the melted wax inside a clean, empty lipstick case. ➔ Allow the crayons to cool, twist them, and draw.

AVEDA

Pots-and-Pans Robots

SUPPLIES: Mix of old pots and pans, mixing bowls, candlesticks, nuts and bolts, springs, and anything else you can find; hot glue gun and E-6000 glue.

I sometimes wonder what the checkout person at my local Goodwill store wondered when I bought a rusty pot, a very used thermos, and a mismatched pair of candlesticks. Perhaps I should bring her back one of these fun guys.

The charm of this project is that it can take random items and bring them to life as robotic sculptures. While every project in *Upcycling* is designed to have a true function, I made an exception here because these little guys put a smile on my face whenever I see them.

HOW-TO: Play around with the parts to bring something inanimate to life. ➜ Try candlesticks for legs, a small pot overturned to make a hat, a lid inverted into the pot so you can stack and glue something on top. ➜ When you're happy with the design, glue the core pieces together with E-6000 glue and allow them to dry overnight. ➜ Add eyes, a nose, a mouth, tail, or whatever else you want by hot-gluing them right into place.

Plastic-Water-Bottle Flowers

SUPPLIES: Plastic water bottles with the caps still on, scissors, cordless drill, florist wire, spray paint.

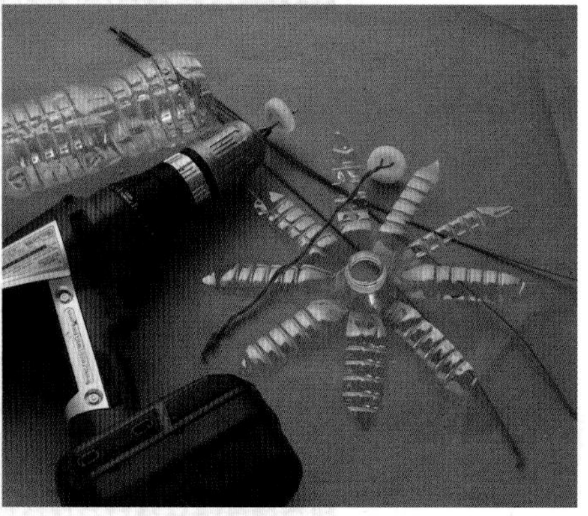

I must preface this project by asking you to not rush to the store and buy a pallet of bottled water in the excitement of making these flowers. Instead, I implore you to visit your local school, health club, or fast food restaurant to forage for the many discarded water bottles sitting in the trash. Instead of being destined for an overflowing landfill, you can upcycle these bottles into the perfect plastic flowers.

HOW-TO: Leave the caps on the bottle. ➜ Poke the sharp side of the scissors into the middle of the bottle, and cut the bottle in half. ➜ Working with the half with the bottle cap still on, use scissors to cut out petals all the way from the cut half up to the bottle cap. ➜ Bend the petals. ➜ Use a cordless drill to make two small holes in the bottle cap, and run a florist wire between the two holes, twisting it tight behind the cap to act as the flower's stem. ➜ Spray-paint each flower in a well-ventilated space and display them.

NATIONAL ZOOLOGICAL PARK, WASHINGTON, D.C.
NATIONAL ZOOLOGICAL PARK, WASHINGTON, D.C.
Yarmouth, Me., Scene on Royal River

CHAPTER FIVE:

Upcycling the Great Outdoors

Fashion designers are—how do I put this delicately—*interesting.* One designer I know was known for his vibrant use of color in his fashions. When he purchased a weekend home not too far from me, he had this crazy idea to paint the bark of the trees in different bright shades. So, when you looked out the window, you would see a blue, pink, yellow, orange, and white tree with green leaves. To me, this wasn't upcycling the Great Outdoors, but more like upchucking on it.

As an environmentalist, I follow the philosophy of leaving things just as they are in the wilderness. Instead of running scissors through a field of wild flowers to make yourself a bouquet, for example, I encourage people to smell, touch, and even take pictures. But once in a while, you do find curious collectibles that you absolutely, positively must have. And in these rare occasions, I say it's okay if you do it responsibly and simply. A leaf from a tree, a few petals from flowers, and even a collection of sea glass from the beach are fine to use for these projects. My best advice for knowing the fine line between harvesting responsibly and clear-cutting: listen to your intuition. If at any moment you feel like an officer of the law may tap you on the shoulder and say "Excuse me, why do you have a trash bag full of seashells and what are you doing here at midnight?" you just may have overextended your visit to Mother Nature's craft room just a tiny bit.

Bamboo Pens

SUPPLIES: Pen, bamboo piece (its width should be a little bigger than the width of the pen), white craft glue (optional).

I'm a hotel room freebies junkie (evidence A: see my hotel soap on a rope project). Whenever I check into my room, I scavenge it to see what freebies I can stash in my carry-on. I'm also that guy that waits for the hotel housekeeper to abandon her cart outside a guest room so I can pillage it for a few extra amenities. Yes, I'm *that* guy.

Anyway, the pen jar in my home office is evidence of my road warrior schedule, with pens from a whole variety of hotels from all over the world. Some are beautiful, quality ones that look store-bought, but the rest are your dime-a-dozen ballpoint pens imprinted with "Hampton Inn" or with some other hotel-chain brand name.

Those pens are great for this upcycling project. The one caveat: all you need is to find a fresh bamboo grove. If you don't have any bamboo growing in your backyard, look around the neighborhood: it's such a popular, fast-growing landscaping plant you're bound to find someone with a grove of panda snack nearby. Then ask for a fresh stalk.

HOW-TO: Snip a section of bamboo that is a little bigger than the width of the pen, insert the pen into the hollow core until snug—and voilà!—bamboo pen. You can add a little glue inside to secure it in place, too.

Bonus Tip: Generic paintbrushes can also be given an Asian-update, too.

CAPITAL HOTEL

Preserved Botanicals

SUPPLIES: Polyester clear casting resin, bottle and jar caps, collected botanicals and items from nature.

I've never understood decorative accessories sold at stores that could be "conversation pieces" if you put them in your home. What kind of conversation are we having about them? "Yes, I bought this at a store so that when I have people over—like you!—we could have a conversation about it."

If you're going to have a collection of something, you might as well have an interesting story as to how you made it and why you have it in the first place. These preserved botanicals in bottle caps are a great way to use saved Mother Nature mementos—a pinecone from a faraway destination, a leaf saved from Graceland, a four-leaf clover found on your wedding day—and preserve them forever.

HOW-TO: Wash out the caps and jar lids and dry them thoroughly. ➔ Collect pristine items from nature: fern fronds, leaves, flowers, pinecones, and anything else you want to preserve. ➔ Place each item inside a jar lid or bottle cap, centering it so there's room along the edges. ➔ Follow the casting resin instructions, and mix the catalyst that the resin came with to create the chemical reaction that causes the resin to harden. ➔ Allow the items to dry completely and display.

BOYLAN
BTTL Co
1891
DIET BLACK CHERRY
BOYLAN

Flocked, Reusable Tote Bags

SUPPLIES: Tote bag, evergreens, clippings, and branches, faux-finish Stone spray paint (such as Valspar brand premium enamel Stone paint).

I used to be the weird guy who brought his own reusable bags to the grocery store. Remember those days? You'd place your groceries on the conveyor belt and gently lay your reusable bags on top to only find a perplexed checkout clerk frantically looking for the UPC code on your dirty tote bags. And then you'd need to explain, "I want to use these instead of plastic or paper bags." Now, reusable bags are so commonplace, when you see someone with a cart full of groceries packed in plastic bags, you just stare and ponder, how could you?

Self-righteousness aside, generic-looking canvas tote bags are pretty easy to find at most craft stores today. While they come in a variety of colors, I find a little customization can go a long way to transform them from dime-store-dozen to stylishly chic.

HOW-TO: The instructions for this are simple: Go into the yard and collect evergreens, clippings, and branches that can lay flat on top of the tote bag. ➔ Place a specimen on top of the bag, and lightly spray a few light coats of faux-finish Stone spray paint on top; I used Valspar brand premium enamel Stone paint. ➔ Remove branch or clipping to reveal a silhouette of your natural model.

Twig Crafting Stamps

SUPPLIES: Rubber stamps, twigs, glue.

I never thought I would admit this, but David Hasselhoff and I have a lot in common. Well, one thing: we're both more famous in a different country outside the United States. Hasselhoff has had a hit singing career in Germany, and I've had an interesting career in South Korea with my books and TV appearances.

Despite my hectic schedule, I always find a few hours of free time to do some sightseeing and shopping in Seoul. Down an out-of-the-way alley is a small antiques store that is my regular haunt. I have always admired the care and attention that they put into wrapping a purchase. At the end of the tissue paper wrapping with string, they stamp the receipt with a beautiful rubber stamp carved into the end of a hardwood twig. The process is deliciously meditative and artistic, and it has made me love the art of shopping even more.

HOW-TO: This project celebrates these stamps by taking your traditional collection of craft-store stamps and attaching them to twigs collected from your own yard. ➜ Start by stamping the cut end of the twig with your rubber stamp; you need to do this so you know what the final stamp looks like when you use the twig stamps. ➜ Then pry off the rubber mold from the old wood base, and glue it to the unstamped side of the twig. ➜ Glue the rubber stamp to the other end of the twig.

W

Leaf-Silhouette Artwork

SUPPLIES: Leaf, computer and printer, paper, Internet access, Microsoft Word, scissors, pencil, two pieces of Plexiglas, binder clips.

The Japanese artist Mitsuru Koga is known for taking deciduous leaves and cutting out incredibly intricate landscapes and silhouettes using the single leaf as a canvas. These überdelicate leaves are sold for hundreds—if not thousands—of dollars a piece and are true masterpieces.

HOW-TO: This upcycling project takes inspiration from Koga and scales down his genius pieces to a more manageable approach. ➜ Start by printing out a silhouette shape on a piece of paper; choose an image from the Internet; cut and paste it into a Word document; and scale it down to the size of a leaf. ➜ Cut it out with scissors, and place it on top of the leaf. ➜ Trace it with a pencil onto the leaf. ➜ Cut out the shape with small, sharp scissors, and leave the stem intact. ➜ Frame it in between two pieces of Plexiglas, and use binder clips to keep the two pieces together.

Beach-Finds Clock

SUPPLIES: Clock kit, cordless drill with ½-inch drill bit, unfinished wood square tray, spray adhesive, small cup of sand, twelve pebbles or pieces of sea glass, hot glue gun, feathers (optional).

When you see some pebbles and feathers on a sandy beach, doesn't the phrase "DIY wall clock" come right to mind? Okay, maybe not. But with one of those craft-store clock kits, an unfinished wood tray, and some summertime beach finds, you can create this beachy, shabby-chic clock, too.

HOW-TO: Drill a hole in the middle of the wood tray. ➔ Spray the entire outer surface with spray adhesive, and sprinkle sand on top until it's completely covered. ➔ Insert the clock kit (according to package instructions) through the hole so the mechanical box fits inside the tray. ➔ Attach the hour, minute, and second hands, and glue feathers on top if desired. ➔ Place the twelve pebbles or pieces of sea glass around the perimeter of the clock, and use the hot glue gun to attach them.

Rock Frames

SUPPLIES: **Large river rocks, standard floral cloth wire 18 gauge weight, 18-inch-long, pictures, notes, or postcards to display.**

I think one of the greatest things to scavenge for in the river (other than nuggets of gold) is to find the perfect, smoothed-over, beautiful river rock. I love to decorate my house with rocks because they're big, gorgeously shaped, and come in a variety of tones and colors that complement whatever I place them by. You'll find rocks on stacks of books in the living room, inside apothecary jars signed with the date and location where I found them (e.g. Costa Rica, December 2007), and even in the shower piled in the corner to make it seem as if I'm outdoors showering off from a day at the beach.

HOW-TO: Start by wrapping 6 to 10 inches of an 18-inch length of florist wire around the rock, and twist it tightly at the top with your fingers so it's snug around the rock. Keep in mind the more wire you wrap around the rock, the shorter the overall height of the picture holder will be. ➔ With the remaining portion of wire standing upright, twist about 1 inch from the top of the wire into a spiral circle. Make sure the spiral is snug enough to grasp tightly onto whatever you want to display so it stays put exactly where you want it.

Yarmouth, Me., Scene on Royal River.

Spiderweb Artwork

SUPPLIES: Abandoned spiderweb, two panes of Plexiglas, black matte paint, white spray paint, spray adhesive.

If you admire the intricacy and patterns of a great, big spiderweb you find in the yard, here's a brilliant way to turn it into art. But before my animal activist readers plan a candlelit vigil outside my craft studio, listen up: only use old, abandoned spiderwebs and never freshly woven ones. Spiders are, after all, our natural friends who devour those pesky mosquitos. Got it?

HOW-TO: Paint one pane of Plexiglas with black matte paint. ➔ Allow it to dry. ➔ When it's dry, spray a light coat of spray adhesive on the painted Plexiglas. ➔ Locate an abandoned spiderweb and spray light coats of white paint on it; the natural stickiness of the web will pick up the paint and become coated. ➔ Bring the painted Plexiglas pane behind the web and slowly mount it; the spray adhesive will help in catching the individual strands. ➔ Place the clean Plexiglas pane on top of the mounted web, being careful to match up the pane precisely. The spray adhesive will bind the two panes together.

Spoon-Plant ID Markers

SUPPLIES: Old spoon, hammer, piece of wood, alphabet stamp kit, permanent ink pad, rubbing alcohol (optional).

If you're stressed, or need to get some aggression out or simply hate spoons, this upcycling idea is for you because you need to hit, hammer, and bang the hell out of spoons to make this.

HOW-TO: All you have to do is take an old spoon and hammer it completely flat. Use an old piece of wood so you don't ruin your floors or antique dining room table when you place the spoon on top and start hammering away. ➔ When it's flat, use an alphabet stamp kit and a permanent ink pad to stamp out the plant's name. ➔ If you want to reuse the spoons, use rubbing alcohol to wipe off the ink. They also make great place markers for parties.

PARSLEY
BASIL

Tennis-Ball Swing

SUPPLIES: About fifty used tennis balls (your local tennis club would probably be more than happy to donate), a 20-inch length of nylon rope, cordless drill with a 1-inch drill bit, clamp.

If I had to pick one upcycling project that is my absolute favorite in this entire book, this one would definitely be it. When I visited the U.S. Open in Flushing, New York, I asked one of the linesmen what happened to all the tennis balls after they've been used. He said once these rubber balls lost even the tiniest amount of bounce, they went to a special room. Correction: all 50,000 balls went to the tennis-ball cemetery.

Now, even I know there aren't enough golden retrievers out there who can play fetch with all of these balls. And when you think about all of the country clubs, high schools, and tennis camps all over the country also tossing out spent balls, it adds up to a lot of bouncy balls heading to the landfill. What did I do? I made a swing.

This tennis-ball swing is incredible because it's comfortable, weatherproof, and really, truly works as a swing! And the supplies to make it are inexpensive and easy to find.

HOW-TO: If holding a tennis ball in your hand and drilling a 1-inch hole through the middle makes you a nervous wreck, use a clamp to hold the tennis ball and drill away. ➜ Drill all fifty tennis balls at once to get this tedious part of the project out of the way. When you do drill, keep in mind you will hear a loud POP sound; it just means you've burst the internal rubber ball. No need to worry, but I wanted to address this since the first time it happens may alarm you. ➜ Measure about 5 feet down from the end of the rope and make a knot. ➜ Thread balls from the other end, and tie another knot when you're done adding all fifty tennis balls. ➜ Hang from a very sturdy branch (higher than you think off the ground since your body weight will bring the overall swing down to the ground), and tap into your inner Boy or Girl Scout to create secure knots.

Bathroom-Towel Picnic Blanket

SUPPLIES: Two bath towels, eight hand towels, strongest strength Stitch Witchery, iron and ironing board.

There are a couple of things in my house that I have a hard time throwing out like bath towels. If you're like me, you have a stack of threadbare towels in your linen closet that you think you can use just *one more time*. After all, their job is to simply dry you off after a quick shower, so who cares if there are holes and fringe at the edges?

If you need any excuse to raid a white sale and stock up on new towels, perhaps this project will motivate you. Whether it's a summertime movie at a park, a picnic in your own backyard, or you're a mother waiting out your kid's soccer tournament, this comfy blanket can turn any patch of grass into your very own piece of Eden.

HOW-TO: I'm not going to lie to you: this is not the easiest project to accomplish in this book. It's not that the technique is hard; it's just time-consuming and cumbersome. Stitching the first towel together is a breeze, but once you start adding more, it becomes this terry-towel monster that can be difficult to maneuver on the ironing board. Now that you've been warned, here's how to make this.

Start by using the Stitch Witchery to combine the two bath towels into one large square. You may need several strips of tape to create a strong bond; take your time pressing the hot iron on top of the two towels and work slowly, making sure the tape totally melts, bonds, and cools. ➔ Then add each hand towel one at a time, making sure to use the Stitch Witchery to bond the sides of the corresponding hand towels while attaching it to the bath towels. ➔ Slow and steady wins this upcycling crafting race, so take your time, overuse the bonding tape, and remind yourself: you only have to do this once to create one beautiful picnic blanket.

Acknowledgments

A lot of brilliant people go into creating a book, and this is a big thank-you to everyone who was involved in making *Upcycling* a reality.

To photographer Jennifer Levy and the helpful skills of our digital processor and assistant Armando Moutela.

The clever and crafty stylists: Nicole Arnold, Vanessa Boer, Meghan Guthrie, and Kristine Trevino and Heather Oberhau for assisting and shopping for all the upcycling supplies.

The business-minded folks I owe a big thank-you to: literary extraordinaire Joy Tutela, Maggie Dumais, Tom Carr, Steven Pregiato, Matt Lefferts, Roxanna Mobley, Eric Brown, Mary Douris, and the team at Innovative Artists.

My new home and partners at Running Press: the amazing Jennifer Kasius, Jason Kayser, Craig Herman, and Chris Navratil.

A big thank you to my friends at NBC's *Today Show*, especially producer Alicia Ybarbo who booked me on my very first upcycling segment and became my all-time favorite producer to work with over the years. And how can I forget the two women I'm still trying to convince to even touch a glue gun? Kathie Lee Gifford and Hoda Kotb: you may roll your eyes behind my back when I try to teach you how to craft, but I know you're secretly rushing home after the show to upcycle all of your wine corks into bath mats.

My product and media brand partners at Simmons Bedding Company, Wholearth Beauty and Bath, Authentic Entertainment, CBS' *The Early Show*, and NBC's *Today Show*. And a big thank-you to Lowe's Home Improvement and Michaels craft stores for your continued support.

And my friends and family, especially Elaine Drebot, Claudine De Sola, Danica Lo, Jules Moore, Merianne Roth, Ken Mangone, Amanda Kingloff, Amanda Schoun, Amy Smart, Emmanuelle Chriqui, Kerry Washington, Arabella Ruffino, Diane Ma, Warren Serink, Bobbie Thomas, Evette Rios, Jennifer Demarchi, Katie Molinari, Rachel Rosenblum, Jen Eagen, Anne Kozel, Lauren Bush, Mila Becker, Rosalind Napoli, Samantha Yanks, Kristen Kauffman, and Lauren Hale.

Index

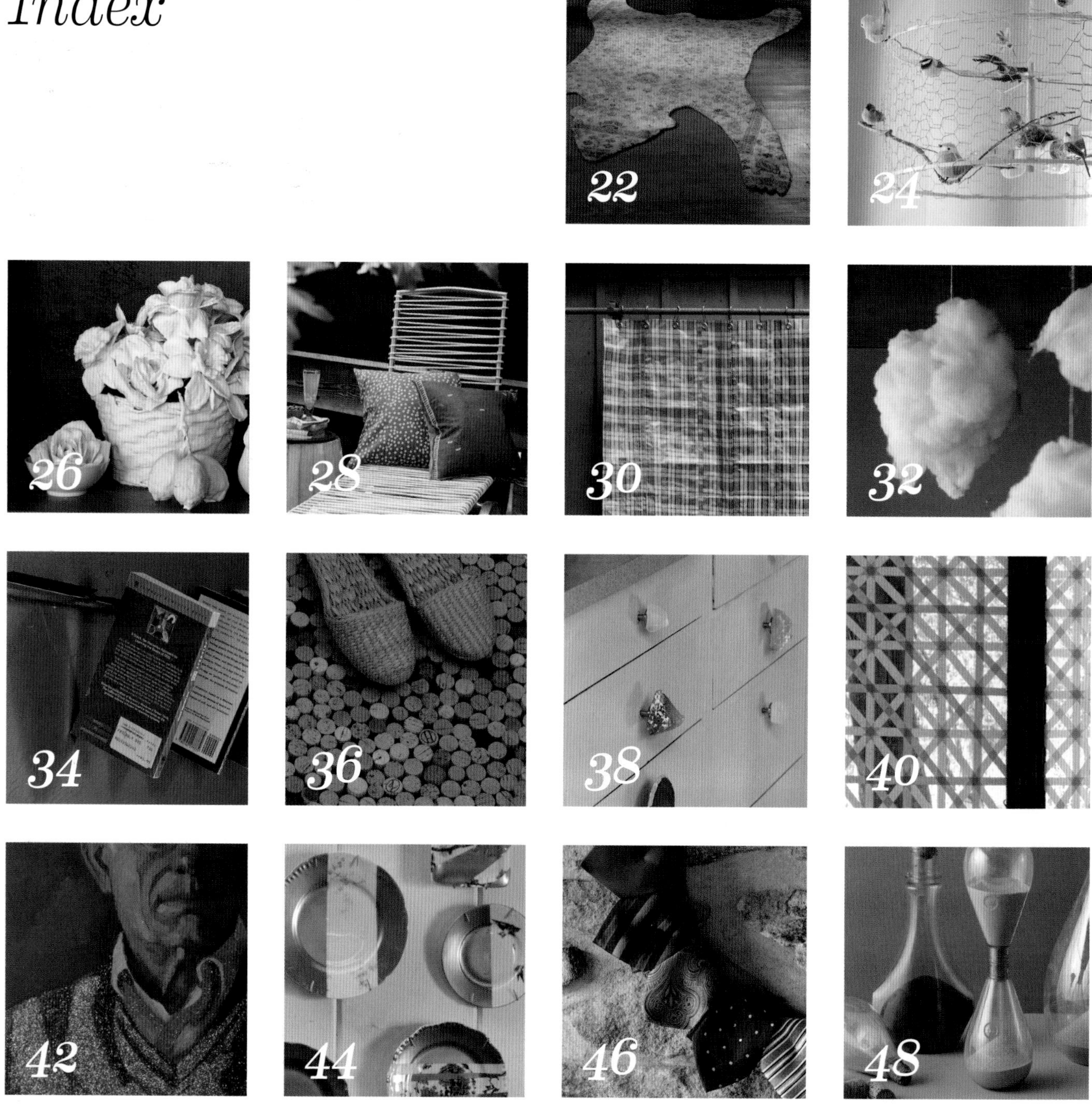

50
52
54
56
58
60
62
64
66
68
70
72
74
76
78
80

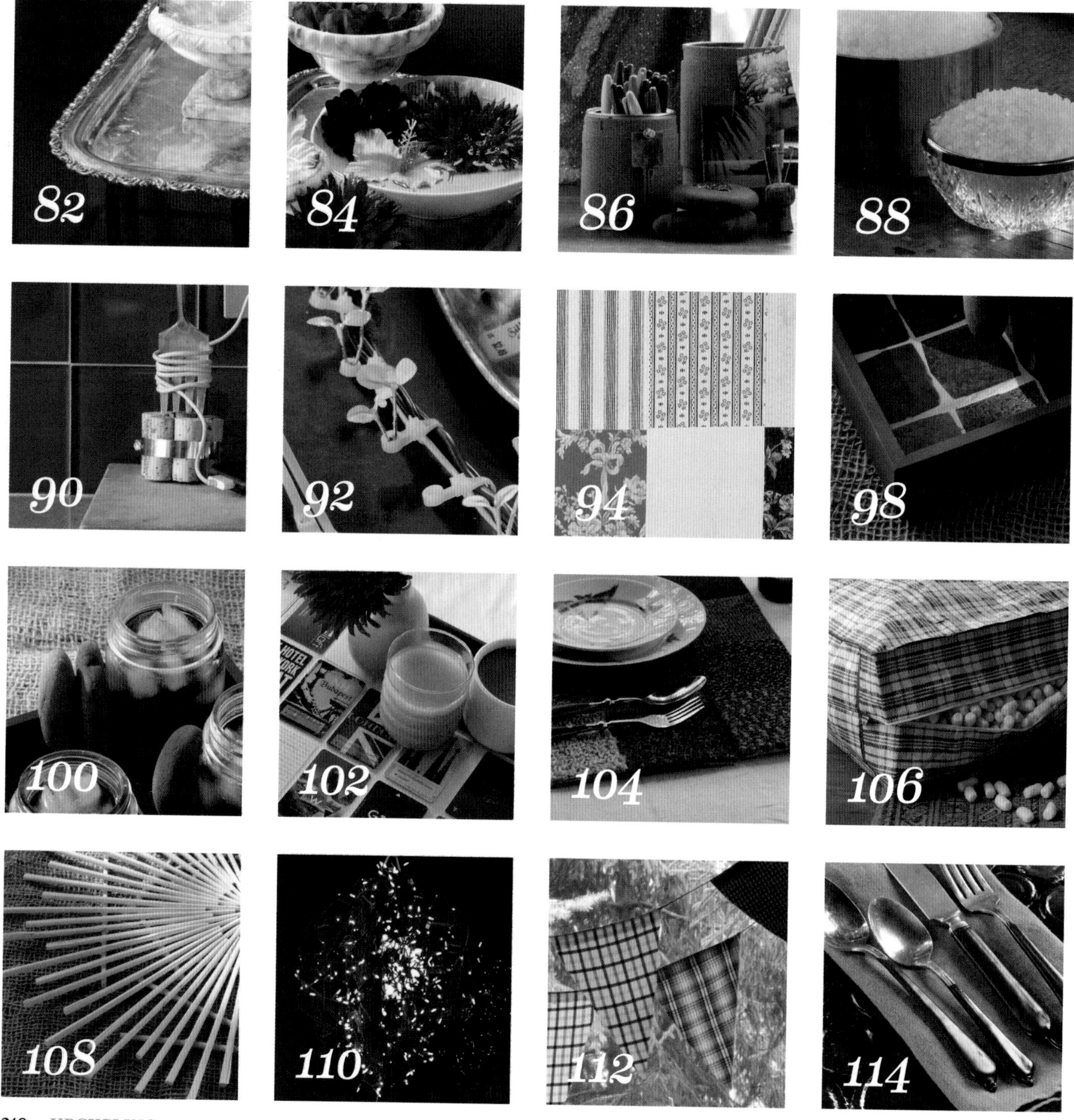
82
84
86
88
90
92
94
98
100
102
104
106
108
110
112
114

116
118
120
122
124
126
128
130
134
136
138
140
142
144
146
148

150
152
154
156
158
160
162
164
168
170
172
174
176
178
180
182

184

186

188
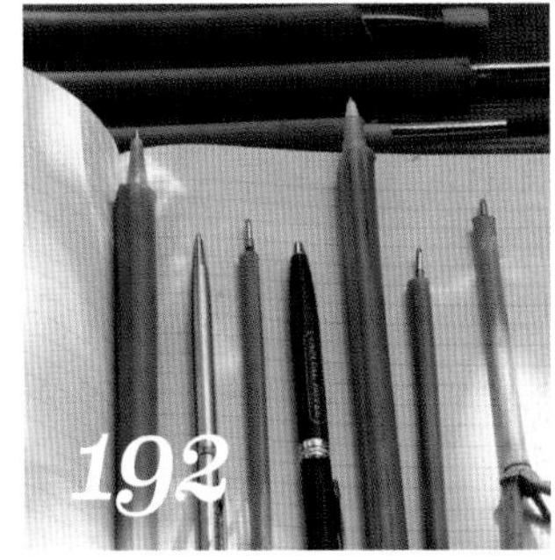
192

194

196

W
198

200

202

204

206

PARSLEY
BASIL
208

210

212

Salt cod à la bénédictine